COMMON

Furz field

13 · 2 · 6

0 · 1 · 34   0 · 2 · 32

D0927897

Mr Smiths land

13 · 0 · 9

Long Thirgoos
foot way

ught

Little Thirgoos

9 · 1 · 32

Jeans Croft
4 · 3 · 30

Conduit bank

14 · 1 · 14

Town Green

Newmans

12 · 3 · 5

Brick-kiln fd.

6 · 1 · 8

Wallnut-
tree fd.

3 · 3 · 10

Bristo field
4 · 1 · 30

Bears   Court
4 · · 18

2 · 0 · 7

Hempplat

GLEBE

Bartholmew

Orchard
4 · 1 · 20

Herods

9 · 0 · 29

LABORNE

Close field

9 · 3 · 13

Eleven acres

11 · 1 · 17

Lit: Blacksm
2 · 2 · 30

Great Blacksmith

9 · 3 · 9

Smith   Bartholmew

R. Cameron

7th May 1984.

GREAT COMP and its GARDEN

One couple's achievement in seven acres

1969. The lawn mower is still going strong. My wife did most of the lawn mowing (and enjoyed it), while I was still working in London

GREAT COMP and its GARDEN

One couple's achievement in seven acres

by R. CAMERON

The tallest *Abies grandis* (planted 1962 and now about 35ft)

Maidstone
BACHMAN & TURNER PUBLICATIONS

Bachman & Turner Publications
Century Building
53 High Street
Maidstone
Kent ME14 1SY

© R. Cameron 1981

All rights reserved. No part of this publication may be
reproduced, stored in a retrieval system or transmitted
in any form or by any means, electronic, mechanical,
photocopying, recording or otherwise without the
prior permission of the publishers, Bachman & Turner
Publications

ISBN 0 85974 100 1

First published 1981

Colour reproduction, phototypesetting, printing and binding
by E T Heron & Co Ltd, Silver End, Witham, Essex and at London

Contents

The glade. The large-leaved pine is *Pinus coulteri*

William Lambarde

Owners of Great Comp

1	Edward Dodge	Before 1597
2	Sir John Howell	*c.* 1597
3	Dame Sarah Howell	1641
4	William Howell als Lucke	Before 1664
5	Sir John Beale Bt	1664
6	Mary Beale	1684
7	Thomas Lambarde	1695
8	Thomas Lambarde	1745
9	Multon Lambarde	1770
10	William Lambarde	1836
11	Multon Lambarde	1866
12	Lady Caroline E. Nevill	1874
13	The Hon Ralph P. Nevill	1887
14	Patrick Heron Maxwell	1905
15	Mrs Frances J. Heron Maxwell	1936
16	Veronica M. Cox	1955
17	Edward R. Moulton-Barrett	1956
18	Roderick and Joyce T. Cameron	1957

The cottage

Illustrations and Maps

11

Preface

In the autumn of 1978, Mr and Mrs Cecil Thyer-Turner, whom we had met at one of our concerts, came over from Stoneacre to have another look at the garden. Not surprisingly, we got on to the subject of books, and, not very seriously, I asked a few questions about the possibility of publishing a book with good pictures about such a garden as ours. As a result of those casual remarks I found myself by the following autumn writing the book on a rather more ambitious scheme than I had thought about originally, including something of the history of the house and its owners, and the story of the making and maintenance of the garden. Most of it was written in our summerhouse in September and October during quiet periods of open days. I then put it away until January (1980) when we prepared a typed copy for Mr Thyer-Turner. I use the plural deliberately as I do throughout the book whenever it seems to come naturally as I write. Just as the garden is a joint undertaking, so this concentrated work of revision and rewriting has included considerable editing, not to mention censoring, by my wife. In the meantime, we have been fortunate that Mr and Mrs Peter Baxter have agreed to come here often enough to take photographs of the garden at all seasons of the year. As I write, some of these have still to be taken during the summer.

The parts of the book concerned with our time here are derived entirely from our own experience. With practically no exceptions no plant is mentioned that we have not grown, no garden or building that one of us has not visited, and in general a reference like, "I built a wall", or "I dug a bed", means that I did it with my own hands.

Neither of us had previously been much involved in historical research and we spent many fascinating hours in the early part of this year in Public Libraries, the Kent County Archives Search Room, churches and churchyards, and studying our own books, magazines and legal documents, and the memories of several people have provided some of the more recent details.

Our searches, I think, reached their peak on 13th March, when 192 years after the 12-year-old Jane Austen stayed there with her great-uncle Francis, we visited the Red House, Sevenoaks, now a Solicitor's office. There we found a bundle of old deeds from which we obtained all the missing information about the ownership of Great Comp in the XVIIth century. It was truly an occasion for "eureka" and I actually used the word to the receptionist on leaving.

We have found XVIIth century legal English quite easy to follow in spite of inconsistent spelling. We have made typed copies of 10 documents in which the phrase "executors, administrators and assignes" appeared many times, so we were delighted to find the exact same phrase in the first sentence of the contract I signed with Bachman & Turner, differing only in the omission of the 'e' of 'assignes'. In general, in quoting we have followed the original spelling but in the case of the Lambarde family name, which was spelt without the final 'e' during the XVIIIth century, unless actually quoting from an original document we have used the modern form throughout. In the XVIth and the first half of the XVIIth century spelling was apparently considered as unimportant as it is in some schools today. In four lines of *The Perambulation of Kent* written by the

13

Rodgersia podophyllum with *Picea omorika* and *Metasequoia glyptostroboides* on the right background. This is the other end of the path on page 29

erudite William Lambarde the word 'Britons' is spelt in three different ways, and in the whole book in at least six ways including the modern one. This book which has recently been reprinted is very readable and well worth seeking out. The map on the cover shows Compherst (cf on the same map Syssingherst), the earliest reference I have yet seen to a house here, although from the position of the parish boundary it is probably either the present Comp or Little Comp.

Prior to 1752, in England the year started on 25th March (in Scotland after 1600, New Year's Day was 1st January) a fact, which together with church registers being records of baptisms and burials, not births and deaths, makes it difficult to be certain of the year when the event happened in January to March. For example, the death of William Clerke, Esq., is recorded on his memorial brass as 23rd March 1611, and his burial in the Wrotham church register as 25th March 1612—New Year's Day. We have tried to ensure that all the dates in the book are correct to the new calendar used today, i.e. William Clerke died in 1612.

We have also tried to be as accurate as possible throughout and where anything is stated as a fact, we have seen or heard sufficient evidence to justify it beyond reasonable doubt, and we have preferred to put everything in the text rather than use footnotes or reference numbers. Some of the sources consulted are included in the list at the end of the book but I have not attempted to note all those used in the various libraries.

Likewise, we are in no way botanists and have dealt with the problem of plant names as best we could. In fact, we found it not too difficult and I even thought of including a paragraph or two on the subject to persuade others of the fact, but I gave up the idea as too dangerous. I have used italics with a capital initial for generic names (genus, pl. genera) and small initial for specific names (species, pl. species), and for cultivars ordinary type with capital initials and in single quotation marks. For common names there seems to be no consistency in the books I have read, so I have used ordinary type with capital initials when their use seems appropriate. Occasionally I have omitted part of a long botanical name if I have thought there was no danger of confusion.

The last Chapter, virtually a list of plant names, we intend to incorporate in a guide book for garden visitors.

Most of the pictures have been taken by Mr and Mrs Baxter, others at various times in the past by friends, and some of the old ones are prints from a number of old glass negatives we found in an outbuilding.

The maps on pages 119 and 143 are reproduced by permission of the Kent County Archivist, and the one on page 83 by permission of the Controller, H.M. Stationery Office. I drew the plan of the garden myself and the artwork and lettering were completed by our friend, Mrs Susan Hulme.

During last winter we often wondered how we could expect to get one hundred interesting pictures to illustrate a book about one private garden. In fact, the reverse has occurred, and we have had to exclude at least as many good pictures as we have used. We then had to decide on plants versus views, and as the pictures are intended to illustrate this garden rather than any other, views have to predominate. After a visit a day or two ago, Marta Thyer-Turner was so overwhelmed by the profusion of everything, that she was desperate to have more examples of the dozens of plants and plant associations, and we can thank her for some which we might not otherwise have included. But I think a considerable tilt of the balance in favour of views is justified, particularly when produced by such photographic artists as our friends Pat and Peter Baxter, whom we cannot thank sufficiently for what I think has been almost a labour of love.

The summer of 1979 for no obvious reason marked a turning point in our history. I was just 61, neither of us felt decrepit, but we began to think of the future of the garden after we have departed from the scene. Now was the time rather than later when we are approaching senility. To use a well-known phrase, we are actively pursuing various possibilities and would like to think of our successors, if not ourselves, celebrating the jubilee of the present garden, and possibly the four hundredth anniversary of the building of the house in the year 2007.

Great Comp, near Sevenoaks, Kent.   July 1980.

From the top terrace

15

Introduction

It is Sunday, 9th September 1979. I am sitting in our summerhouse which also serves as the visitors' entrance to the garden. It is what I like to think of as a typical September morning, no wind, warm and sunny, the lawn in front of me carpeted with leaves from the lime trees, the type of morning so conducive to reflection. There are a few visitors in the garden and, not for the first time, I say to myself, 'Why are these people prepared to pay 50p to see our garden, to come a long distance for the purpose and from all over the world?' Then I think of the pleasure we have had from other people's gardens, and where in all the great gardens we have visited have I seen a better view from the entrance than our own? There is the vista including the sundial and in the distance the Doulton urn, there is the magnificent 50ft yew tree and our own yellow cypress, but I think it is the setting of the lawn and the profusion of trees and shrubs, deciduous and evergreen, which are most likely to strike the visitor, and nearly all planted by us. The smaller shrubs and herbaceous plants ensure interest and colour throughout the year, a small group of *Polygonum* 'Donald Lowndes', with its spikes of red flowers all summer, the Cornish heath 'Valerie Proudley', bright yellow throughout the year, purple leaved dwarf berberis and the upright blue juniper and golden yew, particularly effective at the moment. Beside the cypress is one of the first three shrubs we ever planted here, brought from our garden in London. It is *Magnolia liliiflora* 'Nigra', still effective in foliage, and with such a long blooming season in May, June and even July.

As I often do, in similar circumstances, I walk forward to the middle of the front lawn by the sundial and look up at the top terraces, walls built in the last few years with my own hands, the bottom one only last year, and now clothed with plants of all kinds, all fitting in so well.

Right at the top the two bright green Kilmacurragh cypresses, 10ft high, grown by us from cuttings, frame the ornamental balustrade. What a variety of trees, shrubs and herbaceous plants can be seen from here. As I stroll back to the summerhouse to receive two more visitors, I look at *Rudbeckia* 'Goldsturm', invisible in winter, and now several square yards of vivid yellow black centred daisies, and also *Viola cornuta* 'Alba', flowering all summer and as good as ever now. I think back to the day when I used the most famous secateurs in Europe on one of the viola plants, none other than Percy Thrower's. We enjoyed the company of Mr Thrower one July day in the middle of the 1976 drought when he made a film for Southern Television, during which he demonstrated how to encourage the flowering of such plants by trimming off the dead flowers with their foliage after the first blooming. In my present mood I inevitably think back to summer and spring and how worried we used to be when we first started opening every week; what can anyone possibly see next week? How marvellous it is that, dependent entirely on the weather as a garden such as ours is, it has never suffered to the extent that we have been ashamed to take people's money. Looking again towards the yew, there is a 20-year-old *Magnolia stellata* which has never once failed in spite of its March/April flowering, deciduous azaleas which always seem to give some sort of a display even if some of the flowers have been frosted, and of course the infinite variety

16

Above: Heathers in early March

Below: Heathers in September. Our most photographed view

of leaf, bud, stem and shoot in all the different stages of growth can never fail to attract the plantsman.

Think of our large cotoneasters on the edge of the car park; apart from the berries, which have been overwhelming this year, they can be rather dull and semi-deciduous in winter but a revelation when the new foliage appears, a myriad of upright 'candles' of bright silver and green.

When, in addition to all this, I look forward to the autumn glories yet to come, I feel more like Lord Clive, astonished at his own moderation, and am surprised that people don't flock here in much greater numbers. The marvel, I realise, is not that people should pay to see all these wonders, because wonders they are, but that the two of us, my wife and I, should have enabled it all to happen in 24 years. As I sit down again, I wonder how I come to be writing this book – did I foresee any of this in my early life? I have just been reading in the *Sunday Telegraph* an article by Peter Simple to mark the 40th anniversary of the beginning of the Second World War, in which he describes '. . . a beautiful, calm, sunny morning, the beginning of the end of summer. . . .' That Sunday I remember equally well at home in Scotland. After listening to Mr Chamberlain I walked round our nine-hole golf course in complete solitude and pondered as I had done many times before, often designing imaginary 18-hole courses extending into all the neighbouring farms. Now, 40 years later, there have been 18 holes there for many years, during which time I have hardly lifted a golf club in anger. And I think of another time in 1946 just before I was demobilised when I noted '. . . the Forum Romanum is at once the most interesting, the most romantic and the most beautiful. The ruins themselves, the perfect May morning, the green of the vegetation, the bird song, and my keen interest in history, all combine here as in no other place.' There were, of course, no tourists. Can I also look back to early thoughts of creating my own most interesting, romantic and beautiful domain? I am afraid not. My castles were of the air, for the worldly success either in a professional or business career necessary for their practical realisation I knew I had neither the personality nor the self-confidence. I think I have also inherited from my father a Highlander's laziness which, I hasten to add, does not mean an aversion to hard work. He and I could both work as hard as the next person when the occasion demanded it. It is more a lack of ambition unless strongly motivated, and in my case a great tendency to put off things till tomorrow. But I think I have some brains and imagination, so that, in spite of those other impediments, castle-building eventually prevailed, and my wife and I, when we began to look for a house in London, wanted much more character than could be found in most of the recently built houses at a price we could afford.

Looking back to our six years in London, we now perceive, even if it may not have been apparent at the time, some of the things which greatly influenced our later activities at Great Comp. When my wife found 55 Cavendish Road, near Clapham Common, a semi-detached Victorian house already converted into flats with vacant possession of the ground floor, it was the culmination of a search of a few weeks for a fairly large house which would give us the large rooms we wanted, and also, if possible, an income which would help to pay for the mortgage. It was also to have a garden and a garage. After a year or two, all the tenants had left and we had been able to furnish all the flats and charge

A March view looking towards the garden
entrance and our most splendid, if irritating,
lime avenue

19

more realistic rents. It is interesting to note that neither 55 Cavendish Road nor Great Comp proved attractive enough propositions for any third party to offer us a loan, and we were able to proceed only because in each case the vendor arranged the necessary mortgage. We also borrowed a few hundred pounds from an aunt of my wife's and I think it is pertinent to note that we adopted a strict policy even in those early days of using the money my wife earned purely on capital and never on current expenditure; for example, repaying the private loan and buying furniture for the flats. I have set this down at some length because without the experience it is extremely doubtful if we could

No 55 Cavendish Road, London, S.W.12

have proceeded to the greater adventure of Great Comp.

As might be expected we are often asked how we came to be interested in gardening, which, as they say, is a good question and not easily answered. I have already indicated an early interest in romantic landscape and old buildings, but, as the son of the golf professional and greenkeeper in the small Scottish town of Strathaven, usually called Straven, golf was my main, at times my only, interest. But I had to earn my living, and by 1952 aged 33 I was a civil engineer and also a civil servant, living in London with my wife Joy, a school teacher, and daughter of a Northamptonshire farmer. We had been married on 14th September 1950 in Weekley Church where I sat in the pew frequently occupied by members of the Royal Family including Queen Mary, who visited the Duke and Duchess of Buccleugh at nearby Boughton House.

Joy's gardening experience was not great, but almost infinitely greater than mine, which was negligible. Although I hardly knew a rose from a rosemary I had always enjoyed scenery and man-made landscapes; in fact one of the enjoyments of golf unlike most other games is the remarkably varied scenery of the different courses one visits. The only gardens open to the public I had visited were Kew and Hampton Court where I noted the fine beds of fuchsias. At this point I should say we began keeping a diary recording very briefly what we did. We kept it going with less and less enthusiasm until it finally petered out with the entry, probably written weeks later, for 7th October 1967 recording the 15th Airfield Construction Group Reunion I attended.

The back garden at 55 Cavendish Road consisted of 70ft by 52ft of rough grass and builders' debris, with a 6ft close-boarded fence and a row of pollarded limes along the Abbeville Road boundary. We soon converted this into a pleasant enough town garden, and I remember a passer-by looking in at the gate making the rather sour comment that it was a pity that the fence hid it all from the public. Incidentally, we retained the house as an investment after coming to Great Comp and in fact sold it as recently as 19th March 1979.

20

Referring to the diary I see that we visited Rockingham Castle without mentioning the garden although I remember it well enough; we planted a magnolia; spent a week in Cornwall without visiting a garden (May 1953); attended a garden fête at the rectory, Macaulay Road, where I won the ankle competition; and spent half an hour visiting the garden at Inverewe (July 1953). On 18th August I took the day off for the Oval Test Match, but we listened to the excitement at home in the garden instead. On 31st October we gathered the last beans and tomatoes and dug up a new rose plot in the lawn. In 1954 we went to Kew twice and to Dulwich Park for the rhododendrons, but I think the most significant garden visit that year, and possibly of the whole six years, was to Wisley on 17th June. I can remember to this day the warm, rather sultry weather, and the scents everywhere, particularly of the old roses. I think a significant seed may have been sown that day. The references to our own gardening now become rather more frequent, but the garden visits are still confined to Kew, Dulwich and Wisley. Our travelling was made less easy after February 1955 when we sold our old car and managed without one for just two years. It will be apparent from all this that our interest in gardens and gardening developed gradually, and unlike Gibbon in the Roman Forum on 15th October 1764 we cannot recollect any moment when we made the decision that gardening was to be our life; in fact I am sure there never was that kind of decision.

On 16th August 1956 I bought *Country Life* to read on the train during my return journey to London from York where I had spent the day in connection with my work – and that is how we became aware of Great Comp. Both the photograph and the price attracted us at once, in spite of the additional information that it was a rather large house and in need of modernisation. We are still living in the house which was built in the XVIIth century and has been modernised rather less than most people would find acceptable. It is a friendly

Us in 1957. Note the large lilac bushes in front of the kitchen window

comfortable old house, and very suitable for our somewhat unusual way of living.

We came with the intention of making a private garden of about two acres, and now we have seven acres planted with well over 1,000 different trees and shrubs and many hundreds of different herbaceous plants. Our garden has been open to the public since 1968 and pictures of it have appeared in many books and calendars. It is amusing to recall that on at least two occasions one of our best known views has appeared backwards, one of them strangely enough in an Australian magazine. We have created this garden by ourselves and like all gardeners have had failures as well as successes, with the memorable drought of 1976 marking, oddly enough, the end of the beginning. There is no doubt in my opinion that, in spite of the drought, our seven acres became in 1977 almost suddenly the garden we had been trying to create since 1957. This may seem a long time to some people, but when trees, shrubs and herbaceous plants are all planted at the same time in open ground, it takes several years before the shrubs become bigger than the herbaceous plants, and several more before the trees exceed the shrubs sufficiently in height and shape to look like trees. In addition the garden has been developed in stages by only two people and with extra ground acquired on two subsequent occasions, so it may not be considered so surprising. Almost from the start our intention was to make a well designed garden containing all the plants that would grow in our climate, something which our subsequent very wide experience of visiting other gardens has shown us to be not so very common. It is apparently not often that the love of plants and the desire to make a beautiful setting for them are combined in one person or even one couple.

The very first Great Comp anecdote shows our interest in both, but also our profound ignorance at the time. It was after we had signed the contract that I saw a number of conifers on Hillier's stand at the Royal Horticultural Society's Show in Vincent Square, and I thought 'We'll have a short avenue in the rough grass to the southeast extending from the existing square walled garden. We will plant them in pairs with the furthest pair closest together to accentuate the distance' – marvellously subtle. So to start the avenue I ordered two *Chamaecyparis lawsoniana* 'Minima Aurea', one *C. lawsoniana* 'Backhouse Silver', one *C. obtusa* 'Nana', one *C. lawsoniana* 'Pottenii', and one *Picea albertiana* 'Conica', and in due course, superbly packed, they arrived at our house in London. They were eventually planted in the rough grass of Great Comp. Only those whose knowledge of plant nomenclature is as minimal as ours was then will be surprised to learn that within two years only the 'Pottenii' remained in position, as it does to this day. Incidentally, attractive as it is, it is not a cultivar I particularly recommend because branches brought down by the weight of snow very often do not recover.

Completion of the Great Comp purchase took place on 31st January 1957, and on 9th February the diary records, 'Went to Great Comp in Peggy's car. Pleased with bulbs – mass of snowdrops. The weather has been exceptionally mild. Put in two dozen raspberry plants from 55. Inspected garage and stable for first time.' And so it all started with two dozen raspberry canes of which not a single offspring remains.

Making the Garden 1957 to 1970

One of our early visits to Great Comp before moving in was in September on a very warm day rather like that one in 1939. We walked from Borough Green Station. The last half-mile or so of Comp Lane and the drive of Great Comp itself seemed to be the epitome of the eternal English country lane; past the church and vicarage, high banks on each side giving way beyond the crossroads to hawthorn hedges, and then the avenue of 100ft lime trees leading down to the house. We ate our sandwiches on the terrace looking out towards the Mereworth Woods. There was not a breath of wind and hardly a sound apart from the birds. The early autumnal smells are so different from the scents of spring and summer. Joy can still remember the masses of red dahlias on one side of the square and yellow on the other. She also remembers telling people how marvellous it was to take over a garden which had everything.

The house had been unoccupied for some time, but Mr Edward Moulton-Barrett who had bought the whole estate a year after the death of Mrs Heron Maxwell had maintained the garden during the summer by continuing to employ Mr Fishenden, the gardener. It was, we believe, a considerably curtailed version of what had been at its peak a very fine Edwardian garden with much of the emphasis on spring and summer flowers, particularly bulbs, roses and herbaceous plants, and I imagine meticulous care by three gardeners. Although, as I have mentioned, it had been maintained sufficiently, my impression, apparently more so than Joy's, on that September day, was that it seemed a bit tired. This was probably because the gravel paths were somewhat weedy and the

The lawn in the square in the Maxwells' day.
The steps are now in the front terrace. The
wisteria we reluctantly removed after we came

23

leaves of the large trees, mainly limes and beech, were looking rather shrivelled as they often do in September. Also, as I now know but did not know then, it indicated a paucity of the more interesting trees and shrubs, including evergreens. However, I don't think at that stage even I, any more than Joy, visualised anything beyond resuscitating the existing scheme of things.

I think it will be quite clear that it was two gardening innocents who confronted our $4\frac{1}{2}$ acres that April, in 1957, when we moved in, but I cannot recollect that we were overawed, although my wife remembers saying on the very first morning on waking up (19.4.57) 'Where do we start?'. In fact our activities during the first eight or nine months were much the same as those of any couple taking over an old house and garden, much of the time being spent on the house. As there was no electricity and we had already removed the gas light fittings Joy had to stop working in time to start cooking by daylight, as she found that one of the most difficult things was trying to cook by candlelight – you can't see inside the saucepan for the shadows. We bought our first motor mower, and gardening consisted mainly of clearing overgrown shrubs, grass cutting and weeding, including many of the stone-edged ash and gravel paths, of which more later. As my job was hardly a sinecure and up to the early sixties involved a lot of travelling with nights away from home, and also as it seemed a sensible thing to do, we hired the gardener who was still employed by Mr Moulton-Barrett for about half a day a week. We still have the account we paid for the period 5th July to 21st September 1957. It came to £9 1s 6d in the old currency and included clipping yew hedges, cutting grass by hand, $7\frac{1}{2}$ hours Allen Scything and 13 hours clearing grass, all at 3/6 an hour. For a year or two old Mr Fishenden and then his successor, his son, cut the rough grass and dug one or two of the borders; then from 24th July 1960 when we dispensed with the latter's services we employed no gardener.

A few diary entries will give some idea of our activities at this time (1957).
30th March. Collected car. Stripped boiler house of woodwork. Pulled down ceilings in basement (cellar). Lifted all linoleum.
31st March. Finished pruning roses. Burnt lino. Various garden jobs. Cleaned bedroom. Fantastic number of daffodils – Thousands.
12th April. Joy let ground floor flat to Mrs Dally. First floor flat sublet to Mrs Little while girls on continent.
13th April. Met Mr Sulsh of Hyders re estimate and Mr White of the S.E.G.B.
14th April. Demolished various cupboards.
15th April. Joy's last day at school.
18th April. Moved to Great Comp.
19th–22nd April. Worked in garden, chiefly paths.
23rd April. Electricians started (Acme, Hayes).
25th April. Joy took the car to have the seat repaired.
26th April et seq. Decorating two bedrooms.
4th May. Nyria and Michael spent the weekend with us. Planted trees as start of avenue.
26th May. Work in rose garden and azalea etc. beds. Dining room chimney on fire. Called Fire Brigade at about midnight. It was in charge of Mr Cloke. High wind for three days.
2nd June. Started to cut down the large lilac.

24

5th June. Spent the whole night at Ready Mix depot at Bermondsey and St. James's Park during the concreting of the beams. George arrived at Great Comp.

9th June. Started clearing the rock garden and paths.

13th June. Visited Spadeadam and had a walk round Carlisle before returning by the night train.

14th June. Night at Abingdon at the Crown and Thistle.

15th June. Full scale beam tests at Harwell. Suffolk Punch lawn mower arrived yesterday. Cut the grass today.

Great Comp is about 360ft above sea level and the ground slopes gently towards the southeast. The soil is light, upper greensand, slightly acid; in fact three of the Folkestone beds outcrop in our seven acres. Rainfall is supposed to be about 30in, but in recent years we have had several lengthy dry periods in the summer culminating in the 1976 drought when only about 3in of rain fell from January until sometime in September. The garden is in something of a frost pocket which is annoying in April and May, but generally winter frost has seldom been severe, the temperature rarely dropping below 15°F. On one night in the late sixties the temperature dropped to 0°F but that has been quite exceptional, and on the whole the gardening climate is favourable, the soil easy to work and capable of growing most of the plants we want.

Looking back it would be nice to think that we knew what we wanted from the start, put it all down on paper, and methodically carried out the work over the years, but that was not so. Rather, as I remember, we wanted to grow a great variety of plants, particularly rhododendrons, and proceeded to prepare suitable sites for them with the existing walls and paths as the basic framework. So, although we are inclined to say that the garden as it exists today is almost entirely our own creation, we were not starting with an empty field, but with a walled garden about 40 yards square, several gravel, ash and grass paths, several lengths of overgrown V-shaped hawthorn hedges (the cross-section of a hedge of course should be shaped more like an inverted V), and a small garden enclosed by clipped yew hedges which were in very poor condition. This original framework was an important asset, because at the start we were more interested in the plants than the garden design, and I think it would have been so easy to have neglected the latter in the early stages resulting in much laborious rectification in later years.

In 1957 in addition to the square the garden consisted of a very ornate rose garden to the northeast of it, and smaller gardens enclosed by the hawthorn and yew hedges mainly to the southwest of it. Further out to the northeast and southeast were about two-and-a-half acres of rough woodland and orchard, and in front between the house and Comp Lane was a field of about one-and-a-quarter acres. The large trees were not very exciting apart from the splendid avenue of tall limes lining the drive. The 50ft high yew which is now so prominent as one enters the garden today was so hidden by several scruffy large Spanish chestnuts that we were not then aware of its existence.

It took us some time to learn about the value of shelter from wind and too strong sun for many desirable plants and if we were to start all over again we would adopt the policy of Osgood Mackenzie at Inverewe by concentrating our main efforts for the first few years to providing shelter all round the boundaries with trees and strong growing shrubs. Or would we? With the exception of the lane and about 100 yards between us and the Oasts next door all our boundaries have since 1957 been altered by the acquisition of more ground, and so the shelter belts would probably have been in the wrong places. Anyway we did what seemed more logical then by gradually restoring and altering the existing garden and at the same time extending it outwards into the woodland, orchard and front field. Apart from the rose garden and herbaceous border there were several rectangular beds each with one genus, namely irises, paeonies, michaelmas daises, dahlias, delphiniums, antirrhinums, lilies and tulips. All these we maintained for a year or two, but in due course all have been abandoned except the main herbaceous border, and even that has been radically changed by more or less doubling the depth from front to back. Fine as some of these features looked at the appropriate times it was just not the type of garden we wanted and I think that what is now one of our main principles must have been in our minds even then. We do not wish our garden to consist of different parts designed to be enjoyed at one usually short-lived season. Instead we would like all parts to be of interest at all times of the year, but not of course of equal interest. This is an impossible ideal as it is difficult to discern much of interest in our herbaceous (mixed) border in December, but if you walk round our garden in spring, summer, autumn or winter there will usually be some colour to be seen all the way round from flowers, foliage, bark, twigs and even dead heads, to say nothing of the berries. For one who has eyes to see and a nose to smell rhododendrons and azaleas in summer growth cannot lack interest and they can be interspersed with herbaceous plants like geraniums, bulbs, and the odd winter flowering shrubs, hamamelis, viburnums, etc. Heathers can be nearly as interesting when not in flower with the brilliant coloured modern foliage varieties and the prominent flower buds of the winter flowering carneas. Hardy geraniums alone, in flower from April until the late autumn, provide a wonderful display which can transform even the dullest of woodlands. With summer and autumn flowers we like, even at the risk of spotty planting, all the beds to have at least odd patches of colour all the time, provided some care is taken, in our case mainly by my wife, to avoid blatant colour clashes, and to arrange the plants to make effective use of the marvellous variety of foliage. The general scene can be just as effective as the more usual *tour de force,* and so much more interesting when one comes to close quarters. So we gradually dismantled the original beds either moving the plants elsewhere or in the case of irises (because of weeds) and delphiniums (because of wind damage) abandoning them, at least for the time being. Even today we have few bearded irises and no delphiniums, but I think the time is soon coming when we shall have both again but in rather smaller numbers.

Our main work in the garden in the winter of 1958–9 was weeding and removing hedges and overgrown shrubs. Also during that winter the older Mr Fishenden on his half day and I at weekends and part of my annual holidays began digging the beds to the southeast of the square on each side of the celebrated conifer avenue. This included our very first heather bed which we started by ordering twelve plants in six varieties, their choice, from Hillings. We shall never forget Mr Fishenden eyeing the rather large-looking bed and asking how on earth we were proposing to fill it. When our twelve little heather plants

Great Comp, but could be Gertrude Jekyll's garden

came they did little to encourage us that it would ever be full. But about this time the fallacy of the avenue dawned on us, so the two 'Minima Aurea' cypresses and the *Picea albertiana* 'Conica' joined the heathers. Also about this time a friend with a rather more established garden in the woods across the lane gave us half a dozen large heather plants, and we ourselves dug up a few small seedlings from the woods. So we gradually filled the bed and by such haphazard methods much of our early planting was done, but then came a vital development. In the early summer of 1958 and much more so in 1959 we began visiting gardens open to the public, both the well known ones open every week and also the very many open occasionally for charity. I also went to Vincent Square nearly every fortnight for the R.H.S. Shows, and both of us went to Chelsea. We soon began to acquire gardening books and catalogues, and paid much more attention to articles in magazines and newspapers. In short we were now studying gardening seriously if rather belatedly, and one result was the ordering in increasing numbers of trees and shrubs from many of the well-known nurseries. It is hardly too strong to say that the arrival of these plants forced us to pay more attention to the garden design or at least to their sensible positioning. I began to spend hours reading about their requirements and more hours pacing about the ground inserting canes to mark sites and juggling about with them. In spite of all our reading and observations in mature gardens it is surprising how difficult it was to avoid planting trees and shrubs too closely. Even today when visiting a mature garden I seldom leave it without having measured by pacing the spread of some of the plants. I must have moved hundreds after planting them, any time from the same day to a year or two afterwards, and still found many absurdly overcrowded after say ten years of growth. Nevertheless I

27

hope I can assure future planters that it doesn't matter very much provided you have done your best as outlined above. Trees and shrubs can die or fail to thrive or turn out to be unsatisfactory varieties or too many of the coarser varieties have been planted, and we have found that by removing all these in due course we have seldom been faced with the difficult decision as to which of two equally desirable established plants must be removed to avoid damaging the other. I can also say that much as we have always regretted having to remove established plants, almost without exception we have hardly missed them when they have gone. It should also be remembered that very many shrubs are well suited to mingling with their neighbours, so that overcrowding then matters much less.

In these early days we often planted the trees and shrubs in carefully prepared holes about 6ft in diameter in the rough grass, and as time permitted joined them together to form large beds. What was to be done to fill the ground in between while the plants were growing to something like the size mentioned in the catalogues? Apart from constantly weeding or hoeing the bare ground, which did not appeal to us, I think there are two main methods. These are the close boskage of Michael Haworth-Booth using mainly smaller shrubs, and the ground cover of Graham Thomas using suitable herbaceous plants. We have used both methods with the latter predominating in the larger more outlying areas. Some of our older shrubs such as *Magnolia stellata, Rhododendron* 'Blue Peter' and *Viburnum* 'Lanarth' have been surrounded by the same hardy geraniums for about twenty years with practically no weeding whatsoever. We try to avoid the uniformity of tallest to the back, shortest to the front by having occasionally a larger shrub near the path and also by leaving 'bays' for mainly herbaceous plants. We steadily extended the planted area and I see from a diary entry of 3rd March 1959 that part of the front field was fenced off and we started extending the garden in that direction. The layout of the beds themselves was in general determined by a fairly well thought out system of gently curved grass paths about 7ft wide (four cuts of a 24in cylinder mower) mostly reduced fairly recently to about 5ft 6in (three cuts) which we are finding quite wide enough, but I would still advocate making them 7ft wide to begin with to help ensure that the shrubs are not too close to the path. We also converted all the rough grass to cylinder mown lawns, eventually leaving only the car park to be cut by a rotary machine. All lawns and paths are cut at least once a week in the growing season, and all have been cut at one time or another during every month of the year.

A satisfactory colourful laboursaving garden can be designed using these methods, but we do not consider labour saving to be an end in itself. We rather look upon it as a means by which we can have a fairly large 'landscape' type of garden for much of our seven acres whilst leaving us enough time to design and plant a number of smaller areas where we can grow many of the smaller shrubs, herbaceous, alpine and woodland plants which need and deserve more attention and without which we would find gardening much less interesting, and which are so suitable for the many walls and paved areas which we were to construct over the next twenty years.

It would be tedious to mention more than a few of the developments in the next few years; it would tend to look like a series of diary entries of which the following would suffice:

28   One of our curved paths with a
                                  metasequoia on the left

15th November 1959. Planted two *Ch.* 'Allumii', creeping juniper, variegated box and two berberis bought by Joy yesterday at W.I. Bazaar.

28–29th November. Planted 32 trees and shrubs from Wallace and Barr.

5th December. Replanted various rhododendrons.

12th December. Planted 19 trees and shrubs from Hillier.

19–20th December. Planted Brewer's spruce and *Cedrus libani* (latter in nursery, a present from Uncle Bernard).

12th February 1960. Fishenden started our new vegetable garden.

This was the younger Mr Fishenden, and it makes strange reading today as we now grow no vegetables but asparagus.

I think except for the last part of the front field the making and main 'heavy' planting of the garden can be said to have taken place in the 1960s, and how we did it with me in a full time job we find hard to understand on reflection. In September 1961 we had a second and larger piece of the front field fenced off and in January 1962 we acquired two more acres of ground from Mr R. J. Ellingham, a large rectangular piece to the southeast and a long narrow strip on the northeast boundary which then became straight instead of an exceedingly wavy line. In 1970 we made the last and largest incursion into the front field, leaving only the present car park. The design and planting of these areas proceeded as before, canes marking the edges of lawns and paths and the sites for the trees and shrubs. We did make one plan on paper for the newly acquired area of almost two acres to the southeast. This was completely empty ground which had been used for growing lettuces and beans. We marked on the plan the proposed paths and sites for the permanent trees, and then planted over a

From the very end of the garden by the temple with the
monkey tree in the centre

30

The old rose garden in 1959 with the beeches
on the left. We abandoned it that winter and
it is now the nursery and part of the ruin.
The sundial is now in the yard

thousand Christmas trees and several hundred larch, birch and Scots pine to fill the ground temporarily. Most of these were sold or removed eventually and used for firewood, but we have kept some groups of birch selected for their bark, and a few of each of the others. We intended to remove all of the Christmas trees (*Picea abies*) as we did not consider them to be suitable trees for Kent, but they have done so well that we intend to retain a few. Incidentally, when visiting Wakehurst Place recently I said to my wife, 'Look at that magnificent tree. What is it?' – It was a fine Christmas tree about 100ft high.

Of all the many projects during these years two deserve special mention, both round about the time we acquired the two acres.

We made the rather important decision to abolish the rose garden. It consisted of an elaborate pattern of twenty beds divided by ash paths with stone edges and a sundial in the middle. It had been made originally for carnations, but after they failed it had been replanted with roses, many of which by the time we came were in poor condition, probably due to the competition of beech roots. I can remember the enormous pile of stones which at that time we did not know what to do with. In fact using some of the rose garden and some of the adjoining 'bowling green' we made a hill by first removing the top soil, placing all the pile of stones to form a core, replacing the topsoil and then digging a large hole adjacent to the hill, and using the soil for raising the latter. This became our heather hill, whose curious history since then is related in the next chapter, but the hole which was intended to accentuate the hill and contain ferns and moisture-loving plants was not a success. It was about 6ft deep and, without an outlet drain, in spite of our light soil it filled with water in wet winters and nothing could be grown in it; so eventually we filled it in again with weeds and other debris.

31

The other project was in the square, walled garden. The ash and gravel paths were about 8ft wide and the two main borders were also 8ft which we decided was far too narrow. So we dug up half the width of the paths and brought compost and soil from elsewhere to make the borders 12ft wide. The path along the side opposite the house was about 12ft wide which we reduced to 4ft by covering the remainder with soil to be in due course an extension of the main lawn. After seriously thinking about York stone we got a local contractor to pave all four sides of the square with ordinary 2in thick concrete paving slabs 4ft wide. This is an important matter in our history because these slabs weathered so well to a stone-like appearance, but with a less slippery surface, that the same type of slab has been used for all the considerable areas we have done since. I did not then feel I could cope with such heavy slabs but have now laid many hundreds.

The most photographed view of the whole garden is undoubtedly that looking back to the house from the far southeastern boundary. The heathers which are an important feature of this view were planted in or around 1967 to replace shrub planting between six magnolias which did not thrive in what was then a very exposed position, and most of which are doing well elsewhere.

We first opened the garden to the public in 1968 and the two chapters on making the garden could well have been separated at that point, but I think an even more significant date was 30th April 1971. One of the advantages of working in the Civil Service at that time was that it was possible to retire at 50 and 'freeze' the pension one had earned which would begin to be paid after one's 60th birthday. My work up to about 1965 was mainly concerned with the apparently un-Civil Service-like subject of concrete technology involving much travelling over the United Kingdom and rather dirty site activity, but the experience has not been altogether useless at Great Comp. The rest of my time was on Establishment matters concerning training, and all of this work I also enjoyed. But I had for several years been considering retiring early and in April 1971, after twenty years or so service, I decided to take the fairly drastic step of giving up paid employment so that my wife and I would have to fend for ourselves.

Making the Garden 1970 to 1980

Although I retired in April 1971 the developments to be described in this chapter when I used two weeks of my annual holiday to build the terrace in the yew garden which we now call the tea terrace started during the previous winter. At the same time the lawn in that garden was dug up and converted to a rose garden with a small pool in the middle, and we also grubbed up (a very difficult decision) about ten yards of yew hedge. These slabs including the paths round the roses were the first I ever laid, and like many amateurs before me I was getting quite good at it by the time I had finished, which of course for most people with small gardens is too late. However, here, although I didn't foresee it at the time, I was to have very many opportunities to benefit from this first experience, and not only in laying slabs but also building stone walls. We employed a bricklayer to make a doorway from this new terrace into the old dairy and realised it would be very suitable for serving tea on open days. The cast iron lamp standard near this door was brought from 55 Cavendish Road. Fortunately Hyders of Plaxtol had in stock a most suitable lantern which they fitted.

Before proceeding with the rest of the story I would like to explain briefly the principles we worked to now that we were full-time gardeners. It has not been easy to recall the main stages in the garden development until 1970 even with the aid of the diary and it is even more difficult to remember our theories and ideas of design, but by that date certain principles had evolved which we have followed in designing the many new features we have superimposed on the overall plan as it had grown up to that time. These can be summarised as follows:

1. There must be an almost inexhaustible variety of garden views which will mostly be quite different from landscapes because of the greater detail and smaller scale of the planting, and because of the mown lawns, ornaments, paving and buildings. No garden can hope to equal the grandeur of natural or man-made scenery like the Bay of Naples, the Champs Elysées, my own Scottish Highlands and even our own North Downs when at its best in the autumn. These garden views, whether from the various house windows, during walks round the garden, or whilst sitting down having a rest, coffee, lunch, tea or a drink, will themselves vary according to the weather (including the transitory effects of cloud, sun and shadow), the time of the day, the time of the year and also as time passes and shrubs and trees grow larger and some are removed for whatever reason.

2. There must be, in Brigadier Lucas Phillips' phrase, 'profusion rather than perfection' in the planting. We have tried, many times, to elaborate on this statement, but prefer to leave it to speak for itself.

3. Near the house the garden must be made up of a number of smaller gardens each of a different character.

4. Surrounding these gardens there is the woodland garden. This is for want of a better term, for it in no way resembles any natural wood. With the exception of common oaks, a few birches and Scots pines most of the trees are exotic and their placing is designed to enable many exotic shrubs to be grown. Here

much more than elsewhere vigorous ground-covering herbaceous plants are used, but not to the exclusion of bulbs and many smaller plants such as primroses and violets. Although it must be weed-free we are avid encouragers of self-sown seedlings of any plants, wild or cultivated, that are sensible enough not to be nuisances.

5. We place much emphasis on paving, ornaments and masonry mainly but not always in the more formal parts. In the absence of any natural water we have not attempted to make any substantial artificial water features, as the difficulties and expense appeared to us to outweigh the advantages.

6. We subscribe to most of the orthodox rules of garden design, many of which we seem to have arrived at ourselves almost by accident or too often perhaps by trial and error. To us the fundamental ones may be the open centre, vistas and focal points, surprises either at the end or on the way, and paths gently curved leading one on in anticipation.

7. We believe in aberrations, accidents and exceptions to all rules.

If you ever build a terrace and are as mean as we were about paying for importing materials you will very likely find soon enough that you are having difficulty in obtaining sufficient rubble or similar filling to make up the space behind the retaining walls. Amazingly enough we have managed to do all the terraces and walls we have built without importing anything except some barrowloads of rubble from neighbours. The building stone has come from demolition in the house and outbuildings, from the many stone edges to the gravel and ash paths and surprisingly large amounts dug out of the ground (mainly in the front field) when preparing the beds for planting. The biggest stones we have ever dug out of the ground are now used as seats. A garden visitor has suggested that the one near the road is a fossil of part of a large fish. We like really solid permanent walls, so they are built in cement mortar and pointed with a fairly rich mix of about 1:3. The rubble came from the same sources with additional supplies from abandoned paths.

The work in the yew garden took rather more than the two weeks I allowed. It was followed the same winter by a considerable programme in the front where we had decided to make a large lawn with a terrace at the top, thus putting the house in the middle of the garden. The idea was to create a vista from the front door with steps up from the forecourt to the lawn and more steps to the terrace, which included a stone (ie concrete) balustrade, using our neighbours' trees across the road as a backcloth. The sudden appearance near the road of this rather garish erection at the top of our field unadorned by any plants whatsoever I believe led to some local speculation about our intentions. These works and the associated planting were intended at that time to be the complete scheme, but a few years later (1974) we built a retaining wall near the foot of the top steps followed a year or so later by a 6ft extension of the paving above the forecourt steps. Finally (and I really think so), in October 1978 we built a second retaining wall at the top, 4ft more of paving at the bottom, plus an additional 14ft square pedestal for a Chilstone sundial. All this piecemeal development without an overall plan is not something I necessarily recommend to others, but in our case I think it has worked and the proportion of lawn (a lot less than half of the 1970 area) to planted area is just about right. Quite by accident it has become in miniature our St Peter's Piazza after Bernini. It also

34

Above: Spring at the extreme east corner with a good flowering currant *(Ribes sanguineum)*

Below: The perfect ground cover for large wilder areas – *Geranium* 'Claridge Druce'

meant of course that by extending the borders in stages we were not overwhelmed by all the empty ground needing to be planted during one winter. Yet another benefit: we had deliberately planted the larger shrubs in 1970 too close to the lawn, intending to reduce the lawn on each side by a yard or so which we did in due course. In fact it required the second and unplanned 1978 encroachment of nearly another two yards on the car park side to make room for our herbaceous plants including our beloved *Viola cornuta* 'Alba'. We intend this front series of terraces to be planted intensively with a wide variety of smaller shrubs and herbaceous plants. Progress so far has dramatically improved the view from the front door, and we believe that by making some effort to get colour harmony we shall avoid the spotty effect we are so often warned about. The growth of the trees and larger shrubs at the top and on each side is rapidly making an effective frame for the whole. For example, some of the twelve different magnolias which can be seen from the lawn are already mature enough to play a big part both in flower and foliage. The walls, steps, balustrade, evergreens, golden privet, cotoneaster berries, and the twigs of cornus and philadelphus have produced an effect which has been quite a revelation to us all this winter (1979–80), enhanced by the bark of the silver birches across the road.

I cannot remember that we did any masonry in the winter of 1971–2 but as in every winter, including the 'masonry' ones, new beds were cleared and planted, in some cases in parts which we had allowed to become overgrown with grass, brambles etc, even in the new two acres.

It is well known that Elizabethan and Jacobean gardens of any pretensions had to have a mount sometimes as much as 30ft high with a substantial building on top. So in February 1973, making use of surplus stones and bricks arising from work in the outbuildings, we took advantage of a small mound in the middle of the garden to construct our own mount which I am afraid did not exceed 6ft in height. I built a very substantial curved retaining wall in cement mortar and about 3ft thick at the base which supported soil for a small bed and also a small paved area from which a series of views of the garden could be seen. This was quite a successful feature but when in January/February 1979 we again had a good supply of stones and remembering the 3ft thickness we decided to re-excavate down to the foundation and extend the wall to a height of about 12ft with the Chilstone Coat of Arms built into it. The wall is 3ft thick incorporating within it steps up to a much more elevated viewpoint. We now call it the tower and it serves three purposes, as a fairly imposing lump of masonry, a view point, and a convenient setting for plants which need a little protection.

I mentioned earlier our liking for ornaments but I must say we never expected to see many in our garden. The very first one, a Doulton urn my wife found in a shop in Sevenoaks, is one of the first things to catch the eye at the end of the vista from the summerhouse entrance. It provides a good illustration of one of our principles, for it keeps cropping up unexpectedly as one walks round the garden (surprise). In 1973 we came across the Chilstone range and during the next few years acquired a number of urns, seats and also an obelisk and a temple, and we must not forget the charming little pair of boy warriors. The obelisk we erected on top of the heather hill and often when I catch sight of it I am reminded of the War Memorial on top of Kirk Hill in Strathaven. The

The middle of the garden. Autumn leaves
with *Cotinus americanus* and a glimpse of the
Longleat urn in the distance

temple is in the new ground we bought in 1975 from Mr Moulton-Barrett to terminate the 220-yard-long path along the southeast side of the garden. To complete the record I note that we also bought from Mr Moulton-Barrett in 1975 a ten yards wide strip of land to the west of the drive to ensure that we own the land overhung by the lime trees. Although my wife and I transported all the sections from the forecourt to the temple site, including rolling the heavy columns along the ground, and built the base, I have to admit that erecting the columns and entablature was more than we could tackle. Our neighbour Mr Richard Pierce was somewhat surprised at this time to be told by Mr Baldwin our builder that he could not come to do some work on the farm for him because, 'I am building a temple for Mr Cameron.' The temple garden illustrates several design points. The garden should not peter out at any point. One approaches the temple along the long straight path and finds when one gets there at the very end of the garden a surprise in the form of a small open space surrounded by trees and shrubs and planted with a profusion of herbaceous plants, mainly geraniums, which one recent visitor called romantic. Then one returns by another but this time gently curved path. Another point is that ornaments, in our garden anyway, should be associated with interesting planting. It is of course a matter of opinion, but so often my wife and I have been disappointed when visiting historic gardens to find magnificent ornaments, temples etc, in unkempt surroundings – romantic in effect, but dull horticulturally. I remember much enjoying the wilderness of Highgate cemetery but you would hardly call it a garden.

Mr Baldwin enlarged our drawing room in late 1975, which involved extending the terrace which I did myself, rebuilding the wall and steps, filling with rubble and then paving with the usual 2in slabs.

Then came 1976, the year of the drought. We did not water any grass as we considered it to be more important to save our precious shrubs, which we did mainly by conveying water in a mobile 20 gallon tank and then pouring bucketsful on to the plants – all summer. This could only have been done in a relatively immature garden; it was laborious, but economical in water, and we did ensure that the roots of each shrub got enough. We also believe it is better to water lime-hating plants with hard water than not to water at all in such a drought. Our losses nevertheless were considerable, mainly certain areas of mature heathers where they had been planted on artificial mounds and especially on the heather hill. We also lost most of our evergreen azaleas of which to paraphrase the fox and his grapes we had too many in any case. In one situation which we decided was still too sunny we replaced them in 1977 with hebes, lost them all in the winter of 1978–79 and have now replaced them with herbaceous plants – such are the tribulations of gardening.

We decided to abandon the idea of a heather hill and so we removed half of it to recover the buried stones, and built a 'ruin' round the obelisk incorporating several XVIIth century fragments of windows which we have found from time to time. This ruin is intended to be an attractive setting for plants and not to deceive, but it is sufficiently authentic-looking for some visitors to enquire if there had ever been a monastery there.

One or two points about walls. For the first few years I dug all the sand for the mortar out of the ground in the front. There is a bed of sand about 2ft thick which is as good as some supplied commercially to builders. A lot of over-burden had to be removed and I was sometimes digging sand from 7ft below the surface, so the holes took some filling in. Another way of saving money I adopted was the use of large stones instead of concrete for foundations, but what a waste of stone. I abandoned both these practices for the work of the 1978-9 winter, thanks to Mr Baldwin's little mixer. The first ruin was also the first two-sided wall I had built which is rather more difficult than a one-sided retaining wall. I sympathised with a near neighbour who complained that when he tried to build walls all the stones appeared to be shaped like Rugby footballs. Short of squaring such stones with a chisel the answer is to use plenty of mortar and smaller stones as wedges.

Not only in 1976 but in one or two other recent years there had been droughts and the large beech trees near the ruin began to look very unhealthy, one of them showing an increasingly alarming tilt, and all of them with much dead wood and bracket fungus. Reluctantly we decided to have all eight felled at the same time and I believe we have made a virtue of necessity by first extending the ruin by about as much again in 1978 and then again in 1979, and by making good use of the new open planting area where previously nothing would grow but daffodils in the spring. Over the work involved in clearing the brushwood and resuscitating the paths after the machines had finished extracting the trunks in very wet weather I think it is better to draw a veil, but we still marvel at and are grateful for the skill with which the contractors avoided damaging our trees and shrubs.

After all this tree activity, which incidentally has provided us with about five years of firewood, I extended the paving above the steps from the forecourt by 6ft using slabs removed from the small enclosed garden near the medlar. Over the years I have tried many methods of laying slabs from bedding them in cement mortar on concrete or rubble to bedding them in sand directly on the ground. Only the first method is completely satisfactory, but it is the second method I use today – for cheapness – in spite of the frost heave and temperature movement which inevitably open the joints and allow weeds to grow, but we still wonder if we are right to save money at the expense of future maintenance. The slabs I am referring to now had been bedded in such a good mortar that I could not remove it, and so I found myself having to deal with slabs not 2in but 4in thick – *verb. sap.*

We now come to the winter of 1978-9 which I call the year of the nine projects. I have already mentioned four of them and we managed to complete the whole nine in spite of the severe weather, having started excavations for the foundations of the retaining wall of the front terraces on Monday, 16th October, the day after our last open day, and finishing the pointing of the stonework of the tower in April, having left it until there was little danger from frost. Mr Baldwin, on his own, converted the old threeholer earth closet to an open summerhouse which we call the Lion summerhouse; I paved the floor and the path leading to it. It was near here that four of the large beech trees were removed and we hope that the open ground will be suitable for sun-loving plants such as *citus, hebe, olearia, helianthemun, halimium, escallonia* and *rosemary*. The rather effective hedges of *Mahonia aquifolium* on each side of the path leading towards the Doulton urn can almost be called an accident because they were planted in the deep shade of the old beeches as one of the few shrubs that could be expected to do well in these conditions. Mr Baldwin and I dug a trench 150 yards long and 2ft 6in deep from the drive to the northeast end of the house to bring the water stand pipe to a more convenient place, and he did some substantial alterations in the stable to improve the three back rows downstairs (projects five, six and seven). For some time we had been contemplating paving the gravel and ash path just below the square, and this I did using 150 2in slabs 2ft 6in and 2ft alternately to give a bonded path 4ft 6in wide, and including wide steps down to the lawn between the two large junipers. This we did mainly for the functional reason of easy maintenance, but we were so pleased with the effect even when it was half done that we decided to make an important feature of it. Therefore, in addition to the Chilstone seat at one end, we made an 8ft square pedestal at the other end, and on it erected a Pope's urn. I wonder how many people are aware that Alexander Pope was as keen on gardening as on writing poetry. The last and smallest of the nine projects was removal of the stone steps in the drawing room terrace which I had laid only three years earlier, building up the wall and paving. The 6ft wide stone steps were used in the terraced garden in the front.

At the end of all this as has often happened here we were left with large areas of dug ground with not enough plants to fill them and our visitors must often have been puzzled to see a lot of small plants far too close together and making rather curious patterns. We have tended to use newly dug areas partly as a temporary home for newly bought plants for a year or two, dividing and replanting during that time as appropriate. I think this will happen less as time goes on, but visitors should beware of using our planting distances as a model for permanent planting. But all this ground gave us good reason to have several fascinating trips in the spring and summer of 1979 to many nurseries within about a 30 mile radius, mainly to acquire small shrubs and herbaceous plants, to the number of which there is no end. This seems an appropriate moment to pay our respects to British nursery men and women, both the well known ones and the smaller more specialised. Although we propagate very many of our own plants most of the original parents were bought from commercial nurseries and on the whole we have been well satisfied and are thankful that such a wide variety of plants is still available if one takes the trouble to seek them out. Our only real complaint is the abominable habit of grafting, either using an unsuitable stock (eg, sorbus on crataegus) or when grafting is totally unnecessary; so much do we object to this that in the case of old or species roses we have now made it a rule only to buy plants on their own roots which I am afraid means that we shall have difficulty in buying any at all. We have a plant of the splendid *Rosa primula* which in spite of deep planting would soon revert to the stock without constant vigilance, whereas a cutting we took a year or two ago has produced so far as we can see as vigorous a plant.

Apart from the extension to the ruin already mentioned the only building work we did in the winter of 1979–80 was to have built some steps down to the cellar and some more up through a new opening in the garden wall onto the terrace for easy access between the wooden garden shed and the two little rooms in the extension to the northeast gable of the house. We also connected the water main of last year to replace the existing main house supply.

Above: Front steps, lawn and terraces

Right: Profusion of planting by the temple, and another disappearing path

Below: The Longleat urn in the glade

The garden today consists of four main components. There is the front somewhat formal terraced garden with a wide variety of the smaller shrubs and herbaceous plants. On the same axis on the other side of the house is the square with the ruins on one side and small enclosed gardens on the other – this part must I think have been influenced by Hidcote and Sissinghurst. Continuing on the same axis to the southeast is what we call the sweep with our main heather beds so that all three share a common axis running for about 250 yards from northwest to southeast but with the house in between. The fourth component surrounding more or less the other three is the 'woodland garden' which also provides the vital background of trees and shrubs. I think the small temple garden almost ranks as another component in the main design as it is so distinct from the other parts of the woodland.

In a way it would be satisfactory to be able to look back about twenty years and say, 'Yes, all this was planned from the start', but it would be utterly false, as anyone who has followed me up till now well knows, but I hope and believe that the result of our efforts does very largely comply with the principles I listed at the beginning of this chapter, and we are encouraged to believe, from the remarks visitors make when leaving, that others appreciate it in the same way. I will quote three: 'It is large enough to be impressive but small enough to be friendly', 'Everywhere you go there is something different', and 'There is beauty wherever you look'

The temple garden from the seat in the extreme south corner

Plants and Planting

*'Jock, when ye hae naething else to do, ye may aye be sticking
in a tree; it will be growing, Jock, when ye're sleeping.'* Scott

The 24th of August 1979 was a showery day with almost black clouds to the east. As it was a Friday afternoon I was in the summerhouse looking into the garden and suddenly the sun lit up two Scots pine – often called Scots fir – trunks, which appeared almost bright red against the dark background. These are trees that we have planted and pruned to achieve that very effect, but which we hardly expected to see in our lifetime. An old Scots pine (*Pinus sylvestris*), our only native pine, is one of the most picturesque of all trees, widely distributed in Northern Europe and Siberia, the yellow deal of Danzig and Riga. One of our greatest pleasures here is contemplating substantial trees we planted, sometimes as 18in saplings, even if not quite so nonchalantly as the Laird of Dumbiedikes recommends to his son and heir. In our case most of the trees, far from being stuck in, were planted in well prepared soil and their positions decided after hours, days and sometimes weeks of fairly anxious consideration. But one of the idiosyncrasies of plants is that those just stuck in sometimes do unaccountably well and we have recently noticed some self-sown rhododendrons doing very well on top of an old and not particularly well rotted tree stump, better than some of those we have cosseted for years. What a thrill it is to sit in the shade of a tree that you have planted, or to shelter under it in a snowstorm.

Soil preparation has not varied much over the years. I remove sufficient turf to get started, say two or three square yards, then dig the topsoil from about half this area and deposit it on the other half. Then I dig over the subsoil with a spade, place as much turf as I can get rid of face downwards on the dug-over subsoil and then replace the heap of topsoil. I then dig the soil from the second half and heap it up on top of the first half. I gradually form a more orthodox working face avoiding this double handling say about six yards long and often have had two or three such faces proceeding at one time in different parts of the garden. It makes for variety. Incidentally, old established matted rough grass is not as easy to remove as one might expect. In an area of the front garden this routine has had to be varied as there are seams of hard iron stone about 1ft down which annoyed us when we first found them, but which we now welcome as a source of building stone. There have been many, many cubic yards of this stone which has had to be barrowed to the appropriate building site, and of course many barrowfuls of soil brought from elsewhere to keep up the level. The only difference in the early days was that I sometimes first prepared individual holes for trees and large shrubs. Also in the early days we were able to collect many hundreds of barrowfuls of rotted bracken from the other side of Comp Lane (with the owner's permission) which we used as a surface mulch or dug into the top soil. For reasons discussed in the next chapter we make comparatively little compost for the size of the garden, and we use very little fertiliser. Apart from one bed dug by the older Mr Fishenden I have dug by these methods the whole area of the garden except for the lawns and paths and have worn out a spade every two years. We are fortunate with our soil which can be

43

worked at any time of the year, but a disadvantage with the sand may be the abrasive action on the blade of the spade. My old spade with the blade about half the original size is just right for my wife when I have finished with it. Another advantage of our light soil is that we very seldom have to spend time cleaning tools; it has never been a routine job at the end of the day with us. We are often asked why we did not use a mechanical cultivator. The main reason was our piecemeal way of developing the garden, and we never really considered it. A mistake to avoid is to plant any bed with permanent plants without absolutely eliminating certain persistent weeds, in our case bindweed and couch, which are almost impossible to deal with if allowed to become established in other plants, particularly prickly ones like shrub roses. I cannot emphasise too much the need to start in clean ground. This warning comes from bitter experience, and in recent years we have been prepared to remove shrubs planted by us and leave the ground empty for a whole year or even more to make sure.

In addition to the bracken we have had a few loads of peat mainly used by the handful or two when planting small plants such as heathers. In each individual planting hole we mix the soil and peat with the hands as thoroughly as if we were using it for potting up plants.

As mentioned earlier we gradually extended into the rough grass buying trees and shrubs before the days of garden centres. In the case of shrubs and herbaceous plants we have seldom bought more than one of each as we prefer to propagate our own from layers, cuttings or division, and spend the money saved on more new varieties. This does not apply so much to trees which are not so convenient to propagate in small quantities and so we have sometimes over the years acquired several of one kind. As our plants mature we are getting increasing numbers of self-sown seedlings of all categories of plants, and it is quite exciting to see our little collection of transplants growing in our own nursery. Looking at our garden today we sometimes wonder why anyone should buy a common plant, for example *Geranium macrorrhizum* 'Ingwersen's Variety', of which we have such extensive areas, but we find, looking at an old invoice, that we paid 2/6 to the late Miss Davenport Jones at Hawkhurst for our original plant. I am inclined to think that to be a real gardener you must propagate. I shall never forget our satisfaction, not to mention surprise, at the first sight of the little cluster of roots in our heather and evergreen azalea cuttings all rooted in a now long defunct home-made frame with a bit of electric wire for heating the soil. Eventually it became so easy that we began to accumulate so many of the latter that we were almost pleased to lose the majority in 1976. We still have quite a number but in our opinion and experience evergreen azaleas can so easily become too much of a good thing. On the whole we now prefer the larger flowered varieties usually with looser growth than the Kurumes, one of the few cases of larger flowers seeming to us to be more refined.

Nearly all our propagating now is by layers or division and nowadays most of the layers are self-layered; it is surprising how many genera do this (or sucker): rhododendrons, heathers, philadelphus, many cypresses, some magnolias, viburnum, roses and even a ginkgo. We often remove the layers and plant the small plant near to the parent, and occasionally, in fact quite often, we find

Near the entrance. *Acer* 'Prinz Handjery', *Viburnum* 'Lanarth',
Paeonia lutea ludlowii violas, geums and hostas

when transplanting these layered plants to their permanent position that they in
turn have produced layers which are moved to the nursery. Of course we still
layer deliberately, not only by pegging down or holding with a stone, but also

by heaping some soil over a branch on the ground which we find by chance when weeding.

In propagating ground-cover, clump-forming plants like many of the geraniums, hostas etc we dig up either alternate plants or slice off say half of an existing plant and put it straight into the new bed either at the right spacing or much closer with a view to transplanting half of them next year. We get a tremendous lot of heathers for our own use by taking off self-layers, some of which look like well established plants straight away. Others can be rather scruffy-looking for the first season and we now prefer to put them in a nursery.

When planting a bed I mark with canes the positions I propose for trees and

The glaucous *Cytisus battandieri* and the fiery *Sorbus sargentiana* as background to the Pope's urn

46

large shrubs. I then fit in the plants either from a nursery or from elsewhere in the garden. Sometimes we will have earmarked and ordered a plant for a particular position, but more often the final positions are decided (not necessarily where the canes were) after a lot of juggling with the plants and sites available. Having planted the larger plants, the same procedure, but with fewer canes and even more juggling and often subsequent replanting soon afterwards, is adopted for the small shrubs and clump-forming herbaceous plants. The rest of the ground is then either left empty to be gradually planted with herbaceous plants or even smaller shrubs, or planted with herbaceous plants to make a complete ground cover, or a combination of both. It is always a relief when we

come home with several plants we have bought to find some suitable ground to pop them in straight away. It is not a case of tallest at the back, then medium, then small but more likely a system of bays and promontories, but with enough 'aberrations' to avoid any suggestion of the contrived; and before we regard planting a bed as anything like finished it usually takes about three years of chopping and changing. As with our propagation these methods would be more difficult for professional designers and gardening staff, as it is really a matter of drawing the plan in one's head as one proceeds rather than drawing it on paper beforehand.

Irises, hostas, hemerocallis, euphorbias and
lilies in profusion near the Lion summerhouse
with the Doulton urn just visible

On the selection of trees for a garden I have found that writers seldom consider the role of local climate, particularly rainfall. Even A. T. Johnson in eulogising the ordinary silver birch as shade for rhododendrons gives credit to its thirsty roots for drying the ground. In Kent we find birch grows well and is a perfect scenic background particularly for heathers, but with our low rainfall birch roots seriously inhibit many plants within, say, 15ft radius, so we are keeping only a few small groups. Generally in our part of England I would recommend that only enough native forest trees should be planted as are needed to give some height to the landscape, say a few groups which can be underplanted with the less water-demanding ground covers such as *Lamium galeobdolon, Hypericum calycinum,* and even *Gaultheria shallon.* This does not apply to the common oak which having deep roots is not such a robber of surface water. One of our rules about thinning trees, at least for the first twenty years, is when in doubt, fell, and we have seldom regretted it, but please do not forget rule 7 in the previous chapter. We find that the lack of enthusiasm for Lawsons cypress by some people is not borne out by their performance here so far end, as we have noted, at Bedgebury: most of ours have remained well covered down to the ground and at Bedgebury the different varieties are still distinct even after 40–50 years – with us it is an essential tree.

Although most of our plants have done well enough many of our rhododendron species have since the early seventies failed to exhibit that look of well-being which suits these plants so well. This may be owing to faults in our soil preparation or planting but I think the main reason is the lack of dappled shade from tall old oak trees together with a number of droughts during the growing season. Even last summer which was one of the best for growth we can remember there was a three weeks mini drought in July just when the hardy hybrids needed moisture, so that the growth has not been wonderful. Our sheltering trees are growing and we look forward to better rhododendron growth but probably with a preponderance of hardy hybrids rather than some of the more difficult species and modern hybrids. Visitors' comments on rhododendrons vary from 'I haven't seen any' to 'I have never seen so many different rhododendrons in flower'.

I am intending to grow nearly all our large deciduous trees and Scots pine with trunks clear of branches for as high as I can reach with a ladder and eventually up to 30ft or more, and this is done by a gradual process; for example, I take one layer of branches off the Scots pines each winter, and this treatment seems to suit them quite well. So far as pruning of trees and shrubs generally is concerned, some never need it, and for the others our rule is when in doubt cut it out. If you are still awaiting the plants and can wait for the end of the chapter you will find some of the more unusual trees and shrubs are mentioned there. Here I will discuss a few which are widespread in various parts of the garden, mainly ground-covering herbaceous.

Although we have a reasonably labour-saving garden it would be possible to make a large garden almost completely so by using trees and shrubs, heathers (which once the individual plants overlap in three to four years need only a little pruning in April if that) and the following herbaceous plants (the overall scene would be satisfactory but the close-up detail would be rather lacking in interest). First hardy geraniums (cranesbills) of which first and foremost is *G. macrorrhizum* 'Ingwersen's Variety', the perfect ground cover, tidy, nearly evergreen, scented foliage, pretty little pink flowers, charming little red heads after the flowers have gone, very good autumn tints, and even many vivid red leaves in the winter. It is vigorous but not invasive, and can be allowed to grow right into large shrubs; our only mistake with it was to plant it near small shrubs like evergreen azaleas and some of the deutzias. *G.* 'Claridge Druce' is next but only for the wilder areas; do not put a plant closer to a shrub than about 6ft from the perimeter, believe it or not – don't forget the shrub grows too. Its seedlings can be a nuisance but it blooms all summer. *G. ibericum, grandiflorum, endressii, psilostemon, sylvaticum* and *pratense* and their varieties all cover the ground well though some die down to nothing in the winter.

Hostas die to nothing in the winter but few weeds have time to get established under their large summer foliage. Of the many species *H. fortunei* and *sieboldiana* each cover about a 3ft circle and in good soil are tolerant of most positions except in sun near trees. *Alchemilla mollis* dies down in the winter and can be rather prolific of seedlings but is good to contrast with geraniums. Other spreading ground-covering plants are bergenias, *Phlomis russeliana,*

Eryngium variifolium, Crocosmia masonorum,
and behind the Angel's Fishing Rods,
Dierama pulcherrimum by the top terrace

Hostas and *Viola cornuta* 'Alba' as you come
round to the front lawn from the entrance

From the top terrace

Hosta undulata in the ruin

Symphytum grandiflorum, Tellima grandiflora 'Rubra', *Polygonum amplexicaule* 'Atrosanguineum' and *P. affine* 'Darjeeling Red', *Osteospermum (Dimorphotheca) barberae* and most hemerocallis. All these plants grow well here in ordinary good soil in sun or light shade. To flower well osteospermum must have full sun, when it will flower all summer and continue until the frost comes. The same conditions will suit the following plants all of which are more in the nature of large clump-forming plants: *Acanthus, Sedum* 'Autumn Joy', ferns including the male fern *Dryopteris filix-mas,* the lady fern *Athyrium filix-femina,* the shield fern *Polystichum setiferum,* and a grass *Stipa gigantea.* Other ferns, including the charming lady fern, need moisture if in a sunny spot. For difficult places near surface-rooting trees *Lamium galeobdolon* will put up with a lot and is evergreen, but should not be planted in the better parts. The same applies to the rampant deciduous *Geranium procurrens* and the periwinkle *Vinca minor* varieties. There are of course many more ground-covering plants but these I have mentioned could be the basic ones. Even if the garden is eventually intended to grow a much wider variety of plants an initial covering of these basics would save a lot of weeding, and those not wanted later can easily enough be removed to make room for the others, and in our case transferred to newly dug beds.

I think it is worth mentioning a few recommended ground-covering plants which have been less successful here. *Euphorbia robbiae* although prolific, almost rampant, tends to die back and look distinctly scruffy as well as letting in weeds. *Helleborus corsicus* makes a magnificent plant for a year or two and then seems to wilt. Paeonies due to a disease, perhaps exacerbated by recent cold Aprils and Mays, have not done well on the whole except *P. veitchii. Viola septentrianalis,* otherwise splendid, has in places suffered severely from rabbits. *Acaena novae-zealandiae,* a rampant spreader, is too tender to be reliable. *Ajuga reptans* and pulmonarias are excellent but susceptible to drought.

Quite a lot of our garden particularly the more outlying parts is planted just like that, but for the more formal parts and other places nearer the house we think it is impossible to avoid hand weeding and hoeing especially near the edges of the beds. In fact, although we are more often aiming for profusion and mingling together of plants we also like where appropriate to see the bare earth round the plants and the tidy grass edge. I think one should not be dogmatic about these things. For example, last year a garden visitor told us that a large *Campanula lactiflora* spilling over a paved path needed staking; we did not agree as we liked the effect as it was. On the other hand we find the more vigorous hemerocallis species grown near grass edges do spill over too much and really should be tied back, or preferably not planted near the edge in the first place. Again there are many plants which are much the better for neighbours not being allowed to encroach, for example most dwarf conifers.

There are also some strong growing shrubs which can play their part for years and then be removed either to make room for choicer ones or to leave adjacent choicer ones room to develop. After more than ten to fifteen years' life some of our large shrubs have been removed usually for the second of these reasons. Examples which were all easily propagated by us originally are *Viburnum opulus* 'Notcutt's Variety', *V. o.* 'Xanthocarpum', forsythia, cornus alba varieties, cotoneaster seedlings and even the ubiquitous *Rosa rubrifolia.*

As our garden grows we increasingly look forward to autumn scenes and even winter; a few notes from many I have made may give you some notion of why we do:

13th November 1979. Good colour *Magnolia veitchii* and medlar.

16th November. Marvellous bonfire, what a clearance. Nearby *Sorbus sargentiana* at its best, coppery, different and about a fortnight later than the other two.

19–21st November. Sun, mist, calm. Oaks, medlar, larch, birch, metasequoia, bright red leaves from *Prunus sargentii* thick on the ground, ferns, hart's tongues.

29th November. Visit by Mr Sampson. *Prunus yedoensis* bright yellow, cotoneasters – cornubia berries dazzling, leaves of bullata, simonsii, horizontalis, *Berberis francisci-ferdinandii,* some azaleas, *Disanthus cercidifolius* flowers, *Viburnum farreri* 'Nanum' in heathers (flowers), *Geranium macrorrhizum,* metasequoia leaves on path, oaks of all kinds.

20th December. Rhododendron 'Nobleanum Album' never as good.

1st February 1980. Cotoneaster cornubia berries as good as ever. Late season for winter heathers. *Hamamelis mollis* in front superb.

We have been collecting plants now for over 20 years, the vast majority bought from nurseries, and the whole seven acres are now planted, but our plant collecting will never end. Apart from new shrubs I see two main categories. Small trees like magnolias, *Ptelia trifoliata, Evodia hupehensis, Picrasma quassioides, Aesculus pavia* and *Amelanchier asiatica* are so much more interesting to us than most malus and prunus and I hereby put in my plea for their wider use particularly in medium sized gardens. The second category is the legion of herbaceous and bulbous plants, many of which we have never even heard of.

In this chapter I have described how using sometimes rather unorthodox methods we have cultivated and planted several acres of garden. As it was all dug by hand it can hardly be described as labour-saving, and too often we opened up so much ground that we had no plants available or no time to plant let alone propagate even temporary cover, and so the bare ground soon became weed covered and in some places had to be dug over again. But there is no need for that to happen, and in our way of gardening digging the ground should be and usually has been a once and for all operation.

As a sort of appendix to this chapter we have compiled a list of 40 small trees and medium to large shrubs. It by no means includes all our favourites, still less is it an attempt to select the 40 best trees and shrubs. All have done well with us here, and most are rather uncommon. We do not ever intend to leave Great Comp, but if we had to and were starting a new garden of, say, one acre we would have them all. We would then add to the list another 40 including both more common and more difficult shrubs, and about 20 larger trees which makes 100. The larger trees would include only about half a dozen forest trees, mainly oaks, and even these would be grown 'drawn up' on 30ft trunks. Other larger trees like Scots pine, cypresses, birch, ginkgo, metasequoia, and upright varieties of common trees like beech, hornbeam and maple, although tall-growing, take up little room. Allowing another 40 for duplication the number is brought up to 140. We would want plenty of the cultivars of the large genera like rhododendrons, azaleas, shrub roses, philadelphus etc., say another 100, making 240, which would form the main planting of an exceedingly interesting acre to be enriched by hundreds of smaller shrubs, herbaceous plants and bulbs. After working this out I decided to check by counting the plants in the various categories in our front garden. The part reclaimed from the field is just about one acre, including lawn and paths, but not, of course, a house, drive etc. I was slightly surprised to find the total including the boundary shrubs considerably exceeded my estimate:

Larger trees	50
Small trees	50
Medium and large permanent shrubs	100
Cultivars of large genera of shrubs	180
	380 approx.

I tried, but found it not practicable, to count the total number of plants in this area including ground cover, and my nearest estimate (not including about a thousand plants round the forecourt which are outside the original boundary of the field, and bulbs) is round about 3,000. This appears to make our list of 40 look rather ridiculous, but one has to start somewhere and I believe it is worth recording them as a help to anyone with a similar problem, ie an empty acre or so.

Fuller descriptions can be found in Hillier's Manual and other books mentioned in a later chapter.

Here are my plants. . . .

Acer capillipes. Small maple with striped bark and red young growths. Good autumn colour.

Acer palmatum 'Heptalobum Osakazuki'. Probably the most brilliant of all Japanese maples in the autumn.

Acer pseudoplatanus 'Prinz Handjery'. Magnificent in the spring when the young leaves are apricot-coloured, changing to yellowish grey-green. 'Brilliantissimum' is similar.

Berberis valdiviana. Large upright evergreen. Leaves like a smooth-leaved holly, yellow flowers in drooping racemes.

Berberis verruculosa. Compact evergreen. Small shiny dark green prickly leaves, white underneath. Yellow rather charming solitary flowers.

Chamaecyparis lawsoniana 'Kilmacurragh'. Good shade of rich green making a narrow column.

Cornus alba 'Spaethii'. Bright golden variegated leaves. Red twigs in winter.

Cornus kousa. Tiered branches, covered with 'flowers' on erect stalks on the spreading branches, spectacular for weeks and good autumn colour.

Corylus maxima 'Purpurea'. The purple nut.

Cotinus americanus. With us in 1979 striking in flower for about one month and brilliant in autumn colour for several weeks.

Erica arborea 'Alpina'. Bright fresh green hardy tree heath. Old plants can be pruned to the ground if necessary.

Eucryphia x nymansensis 'Nymansay'. Large upright evergreen completely covered with flowers in August 1978, hardly any in 1979, so we hope it loses

From the top terrace. *Decaisnea
fargesii* in the centre

Birches and bergenias. The narrow path
leading from the long northeastern boundary

Roses by the tea terrace

Pampas grass between the tulip
tree and catalpa

that habit. We saw them at Nymans recently, 40ft high or more, magnificent against a clear blue sky.

Evodia hupehensis. Spreading tree, flowering in late August, like a much more refined elder.

Genista aetnensis. Large long-lived broom, an elegant shrub, free-flowering in July.

Genista cinerea or *genista tenera.* Two large shrubs which resemble one another with denser foliage than *aetnensis.* Completely covered with golden yellow flowers in June and July, *cinerea* being rather the earlier of the two.

Hamamelis mollis. Large shrub with hazel-like foliage, sweetly scented yellow frost-resistant flowers in mid winter. There are several other varieties.

Magnolia x loebneri 'Leonard Messel'. Tall shrub or small tree, flowers like stellata but pink.

Magnolia x loebneri 'Merrill'. Pure white tulip-shaped flowers. Ours did splendidly for several years, then suffered badly in the cold springs of 1976 and 1977, and from coral spot fungus, so much so that I cut it to the ground. It is now growing vigorously. It was almost my favourite of our magnolias.

Magnolia x proctoriana. Another very floriforous shrub or small tree with pure white flowers in April.

Mahonia 'Charity'. Hybrid of the rather tender *lomarifolia* and the hardy *japonica.* Dense clusters of yellow flowers in early winter. There are some splendid tall specimens in the Savill Garden, Windsor Great Park.

Mahonia japonica. A more rounded shrub with much more lax racemes of yellow very sweetly scented flowers. Not to be confused with *M. bealei* which has short, stiff, erect racemes.

Malus tschonoskii. Strong growing tree of erect conical habit. Poor flowers, magnificent early autumn colour. Good boundary tree.

x Osmarea 'Burkwoodii'. Bi-generic hybrid evergreen. Covered with small white fragrant flowers in spring.

Picea omorika. Tall pagoda-shaped tree with glaucous undersides of leaves, better for most gardens than a Christmas tree.

Ptelea trifoliata. Small tree. Spectacular clusters of fruits something like honesty but smaller, which last in good years from July to October. There is also a variety 'Aurea' with yellow leaves.

Quercus robur 'Fastigiata'. The common oak, but growing like a Lombardy poplar. Good for the boundary.

Rosa rubrifolia. Glaucous purple leaves and very good hips. Seeds itself prolifically here. Its foliage seems to go well with any other colour, even fiery azaleas, both in the garden and in the house. Although it is a large shrub rose its slender growth enables it to be tucked in between other shrubs or large herbaceous plants.

Rubus tridel 'Benenden'. Large vigorous thornless shrub often thought by garden visitors to be an early flowering single white rose. Sometimes slow to start, but once established very fast growing. In fact we have had to remove two after about seven years' growth.

56 *Viburnum x hillieri* 'Winton', *Gillenia trifoliata*
Hostas, Geums and *Viola cornuta* 'Alba'

Sorbaria aitchisonii. Elegant pinnate leaves. Large creamy-white panicles in August. More refined than *S. arborea* and not so suckering.

Sorbus hupehensis. Chinese rowan with white pink-tinged fruits and good autumn colour. Also a good boundary tree.

Sorbus sargentiana. Large sticky crimson buds, tropical looking young growth, large pinnate leaves, magnificent autumn colour.

Staphylea colchica. Strong-growing shrub. White flowers for several weeks in May.

Styrax obassia or *Halesia monticola.* Related trees quite different in leaf. Both have snowdrop-like flowers. I could not decide which to leave out of the list. There are also *Styrax japonica* and *Styrax hemsleyana,* equally good trees.

Syringa x josiflexa 'Bellicent'. An unusual lilac with large panicles of rose pink flowers. Long blooming period.

Taxus baccata 'Semperaurea'. Slow growing. The best golden yew I have seen for all-the-year colour.

Viburnum x bodnantense 'Dawn'. Large shrub of stiff upright habit. Fragrant deep pink flowers from October to March depending on the weather.

Viburnum x hillieri 'Winton'. Interesting foliage. Very refined creamy flowers in June.

Viburnum opulus 'Compactum'. Slow growing guelder rose. One of our best berrying shrubs.

Viburnum plicatum 'Lanarth'. Horizontal branches covered with white lacecap flowers on the upper side.

Weigela 'Looymansii Aurea'. Yellow leaves. Does well in light shade.

In choosing these plants many of our favourites have been omitted either because they are well known or rather tender or otherwise difficult with us, and we have also omitted the host of spectacular cultivars of the large genera like rhododendron. Please do not forget that you have been asked to include another 40, and so on. A garden based on these types of plants will help ensure that the answer to a frequently asked question we get here, 'When is the best time to see your garden?', will be 'There isn't a best time'. I usually give a supplementary answer concerning our garden here that the most spectacular time for colour is probably the end of May and beginning of June when the azaleas are possibly at their peak and overlapping with rhododendrons and the earlier summer flowering shrubs. If I had to be pinned down to one time in the year I would probably choose that great fortnight which includes the latter half of Wimbledon, Henley Royal Regatta and the Open Golf Championship, the first half of July. To us there are few things in the whole wide world to surpass our own garden then on a slightly cloudy windless day after rain, and the sun when it does appear is at its warmest. Everything, and particularly the herbaceous plants, at the height of its growth, lush with no suggestion of tiredness, mingling together flowers, scents and foliage, bees, birds and butterflies, cloud patches in a blue sky and us sitting there enjoying it all. But what a lot would be missed; there are perfect mellow days in September and October, and even November, in fact in suitable weather the garden is at its 'best' at almost any time of the year.

Above: *Stipa gigantea*

Below: Three varieties of *Berberis thunbergii,* and *Rosa ecae*

The front steps, lawn and terraces. Comp Lane runs between us and the woods beyond

"I don't know how you do it"

In other words, how can two people manage to keep such a large area and so many plants so well maintained? It is a sort of rhetorical question, often put to us by visitors on leaving and we usually feel suitably pleased. We work hard, but certainly no harder than the self-employed builders I have worked alongside, and although our seven-day-week regime has included slogging away at digging new front beds at seven in the evening in full view of commuters coming back from the station, it also includes hour-long tea breaks on a sunny afternoon to say nothing of lying in bed at 7.45 on a slushy winter morning thinking (occasionally) of a former commuter who now has 'something better to do'. As a matter of interest I go on working late because somehow I am often at my best then, and seem to achieve twice as much in the last hour as I did in the first. In short, and all things considered, we think the garden could be maintained easily by two full-time gardeners working a normal five-day week, and if this seems improbable or to some even incredible then we must look for the answer to our methods, and to one important matter which we can take no credit for, namely our soil. Unless it is actually pouring with rain or the ground is frozen solid there is hardly a day in the year when we cannot work outside. This means we can do during the winter much of the work that in some gardens would have to wait until the spring.

I do not find it at all easy to put on paper our maintenance philosophy, but I will try. My wife and I are, I think, perfectionists, that is to say all the plants should be healthy, there should be no weeds, tidy edges, well mown lawns free of weeds, deadheading (but not always by any means), plants staked as required (which is not very often), fallen leaves removed daily from lawns until mid September etc, etc, but I think we also accept Browning's dictum:

> 'Ah, but a man's reach should exceed his grasp,
> Or what's a heaven for?'

And just as in all great enterprises the successful outcome can never be certain, so in a more modest venture like ours, especially where one is dealing with living things, the best one can hope for is to say with Addison,

> 'Tis not in mortals to command success,
> But we'll do more, Sempronius; we'll deserve it'.

If all this sounds rather pretentious I might put it another way. Supposing a private garden like ours had sufficient staff to keep it in a state of complete perfection then it would be impossible to find enough work for the staff during the six months from October to March, that is it would be neither a practical nor a desirable proposition for people like us to contemplate. So our garden is never quite as tidy as we would like it to be, but in spite of that many visitors make remarks like, 'Not a weed to be seen', and after all if that is a general impression the visitor gets there cannot be much wrong with our maintenance.

Covering the ground round the trees and larger shrubs with plants like hardy geraniums undoubtedly abolishes weeds, and many substantial areas of our garden are so planted; but they sometimes tend to encroach and even overwhelm young slow-growing shrubs. Instead of making a purpose journey with

61

shears which I used to do I often notice it when walking round the garden, and I step in and trample round to completely flatten the geranium for about 1ft all round the shrub. As it is done in the growing season you hardly notice it a day or two later. This is an example of one of our methods which may or may not be labour saving – I don't know. But we certainly get a lot of work done like weeding, pruning and deadheading by stopping in passing for a few minutes during a walk round the garden.

We have recently had a discussion with an experienced friend from Essex who doubts the advantage of ground-cover plants against the moisture and nutrients they themselves use, and thus on balance deprive the trees and shrubs. This is a point which may well depend on all the many things which affect the growth of any particular species, and we can only say that we have never suspected any detrimental effect from say *Geranium macrorrhizum* used as ground cover; in fact more often it is 'The dog it was that died', that is in full sun round the base of trees like Scots pine and birch even vigorous ground cover can fail to thrive.

Canon Ellacombe had a decided affection for some weeds and wrote that 'A weed is but a good plant in the wrong place'. Our policy is to aim for a garden entirely free from weeds. However, many of the plants we cherish would have been regarded by the Canon's contemporaries as weeds and not allowed anywhere in the garden, for example, the ordinary self-sown wild foxglove in all its shades including white which we nevertheless have also to consider as a weed when the seedlings come up in their hundreds in the wrong places. The same thing applies to plants like Herb Robert and other native geraniums, dog daisies, certain hypericums, teasles, ivy-leaved toad flax, violets, and many less prolific genera, which all help to cover the ground – but I must stop using that phrase! For all that there can be no place for such prolific and rampant weeds as nettles, stinging and dead, ordinary grass, dandelions, thistles, docks, ordinary buttercups and daisies (regretfully), willowherb or the rampant perennials like couch, ground elder (which thankfully we've never had), bindweed, and a special weed of ours called blue sow thistle. Which reminds me of a visit, in our early days when we were driven almost to distraction by our blue sow thistle (*Lactuca bourgaei*), to a garden in south-east Kent where we saw a whole border of it in full bloom, and very charming it is with its pale mauve flower on 3ft stems over lush foliage. We were sorely tempted to ask the owner if he knew what trouble he might be letting himself in for, but managed to resist. The plant has roots as rampant as couch but so brittle that it is even more difficult to get rid of. I think I should say how we came to inflict this pest upon ourselves – my wife agrees that it was probably the worst day's gardening she ever did. She found in the paddock a nice big heap of what looked like good compost and proceeded to spread several barrowloads in various parts of the garden. In fact it was mainly the blue sow thistle which had been dumped by the farmer who had rented the field for some years, and we have still not eradicated it more than 20 years later. In the past we have used Paraquat to control large areas we have been unable to cultivate, and we still use it to some extent in April and early May in places where the effect will not be too obtrusive, as it does help to keep control when suddenly everything seems to be growing at once. We hope very soon not to need to use it at all. We also use selective weedkiller mainly against nettles and bindweed, and sometimes buttercups.

62

When weeding the beds we very seldom cart away any weeds to a compost heap, apart from such as couch and nettles. Instead we use three methods. If as has often happened recently planted beds have been neglected from November to early March because of other work, such as digging new beds or building, then there has to be a mad rush to get round in time for opening in May. The weeds will often be as thick as a lawn. I either turn it in with a spade, or more likely I dig a small hole and fill it with weeds either by skimming off with a spade (we call this scooping and burying), or handweeding, usually both. Then having covered the weeds in the hole with soil I dig another one say a couple of yards away, and so on. This seems the quickest way to do it; there is no barrowing, it avoids taking away any of the soil which sooner or later has to be replaced, and it supplies green manure. The second method is handweeding with the weeds deposited either in small heaps as unobtrusive as possible, or thrown into areas of the coarser ground-cover plants (here we go again), particularly near the perimeter of shrubs, a similar effect to the above trampling. These methods may appear to be rather crude, but we have used them for many years and it is surprising how inconspicuous the heaps of weeds can be. Incidentally in the past we have usually managed to dispose of weeds like couch either by burying deeply in one of our many 'holes' or by making a very large heap and applying a strong dose of sulphate of ammonia. The couch then succumbs in the middle and the surface is easily enough removed to start another heap. I mention this because we are most reluctant to burn anything which can be returned to the soil – in general only bindweed and brushwood. Thirdly, and we hope the normal method as the garden matures, a combination of hoeing with a Wilkinson's Swoe and handweeding as required close into the plants. Even here we manage to throw some of the weeds into the undergrowth. Please do not understand from this that all our garden is intended to be a sort of jungle. On the contrary in the central parts such as the square, front terraces, ruins, heather beds etc, our ideal is to have no weeds at all and keep it all meticulously tidy. We still encourage self-sown seedlings, but usually transfer them to our nursery or an appropriate site.

Next to weeding the biggest summer job is to keep the lawns and edges in good condition. We are often complimented on the condition of the lawns although they are merely the ordinary meadows cut short, in fact all the lawns and paths in the two acres bought in 1962 are derived from the weeds which grew in the empty ground. We get rid of broad-leaved weeds with a thorough treatment with a selective weedkiller in the spring, and in places as required occasionally during the summer. We use a 4-gallon knapsack sprayer. Clover we tolerate even if it does annoy us for the short time it is in bloom. The grass is cut regularly with a 24in cylinder machine which I do not sit on. I put this in because the third most frequently asked question (after 'How old is the house?' and 'How long does it take you to cut the grass?') is 'Do you sit on it?' It takes about $3\frac{1}{2}$ hours. I use the box only in May and early June and later if the grass is rather long and wet; not using the box is mainly to save labour, but I think it helps a little to feed the lawn as long as the conditions are right, ie, grass dry and not too long. When I do use the box I usually manage to find a place round a shrub to tip it. We have no fixed day for cutting the grass, but have managed to avoid cutting on a Sunday. The $3\frac{1}{2}$ hours are often spread over several days.

We also cut the grass during the winter if the weather has been mild and we get some reasonable cutting conditions; our light soil helps here and we have cut grass in every calendar month in the year. My wife does all the edges with an Andrews Spin Trim, an essential machine at Great Comp, which is not surprising when you think we have about two miles of edges to trim. They are done every week, but as with grass cutting you have to catch the edges while they are short enough and dry enough for the machine to move quickly and for the clippings not to look untidy as they fall. We wonder why this machine or a similar one is not used more widely in large gardens and public parks.

I have found that pruning shrubs as they become mature and young trees is a much bigger task than I had ever envisaged; it includes carrying the prunings to a central bonfire site. For economy we could do with about three bonfire sites, but this is not possible now that the whole garden is so intensively planted. Of what might be called routine pruning we do very little, only a few hybrid tea roses, the yew hedge and one or two bits of boundary hedge, and a light clipping of the summer flowering heathers in April. This routine pruning takes no more than about four days using hand shears throughout. Another type of essential pruning which is becoming more frequent is to keep paths free of overhanging branches which become particularly obstructive after heavy rain in midsummer.

We are in no doubt that no plant should be allowed to suffer from lack of water, but we are a little coy about watering, feeling almost guilty and always do it unobtrusively and pack the hosepipe away if the public is about. The guilt we feel is not of a criminal nature as we pay for every cubic metre that we use; it is because we feel that correct planting and siting should ensure that the majority of plants should need no artificial watering in most years in our climate. One, admittedly minor, criticism we make of some of the large gardens in recent years has been the obtrusive appearance of standpipes all over the place. In a drought we water young individual shrubs, particularly shallow-rooted ones like rhododendrons, by throwing on a bucket or two to each, but in general we are trying to confine watering with a hosepipe to the front garden and the ruins and even there not much in most years. In short we water where necessary, but think it should be exceptional rather than the rule.

Whether it is just a matter of luck or because the wide variety of our plants encourages some sort of a balance between pests and predators I do not know. I do know that we bought a small bottle of Sybol shortly after we came in 1957 and did not have to replace it until last year. I often use my finger and thumb against aphis in passing. One of the most remarkable sights I have ever seen in this garden was in 1976 when a large ornamental artichoke was covered with blackfly one day, with ladybirds the next, and by the next with nothing. Whilst on the subject of spraying I should mention that we have only a few fruit trees which I am afraid have to fend for themselves. This leads me to tell about one of our mistakes. When we bought the two acres we decided to have a row of fruit trees in full sun along the southeast boundary. After a few years we decided it wasn't worth while for us to try to grow fruit when we are surrounded by fruit farmers willing to sell us a box or two as required, so we dug the trees up and replaced them with ornamental trees and shrubs, which explains why our southeast boundary is still rather lacking in mature shrubs, but it is coming

64

on. We would grow vegetables if we found we could not buy good ones locally, but it would be at the expense of something else. At the moment the only vegetable we grow is asparagus.

Although we have not many old large trees the ones we have are mainly very tall common lime and magnificent as ours are we would not recommend them for anyone considering planting trees in a garden. They sucker badly round the base (needing but not getting about one day's work every year), suffer badly from aphis in some years, are very shallow rooted and therefore greedy, and have a most irritating habit of shedding leaves from July onwards. From about mid-September we actually like to see the leaves lying on the grass, but not during the summer. We have never made a great thing about clearing up leaves, and have no special equipment; we usually wait until the wind blows them into various corners and then lift them and either place them round nearby shrubs or take them away in a barrow to put round other shrubs. In summer I sometimes use the box on the mower to clear the leaves when I wouldn't otherwise have done so. By the way, if you are tidy-minded, do not grow any broad-leaved evergreen trees near a lawn – they drop their leaves in midsummer.

Staking is something we are so averse to that we have abandoned temporarily plants like delphiniums. We do not like the stakes to be visible, or the plants to look as if they have been tied, or to see plants meticulously surrounded by twigs even if we know all will be hidden in a few weeks. At the moment we depend upon the fact that many herbaceous plants which would otherwise need staking will support each other, and we place certain plants, eg *Euphorbia sikkimensis, Campanula lactiflora, Gillenia trifoliata, Cimicifuga* and tall lilies like *pardalinum* near or among shrubs such as azaleas, viburnums and shrub roses. There are also happy accidents – we would never have thought of planting *Campanula lactiflora* within a foot of a *Prunus padus,* but when it put itself there and thrived exceedingly how useful the trunk is as a stake. Nevertheless, we are not content with our present methods which too often entail rushing around putting in a few stakes at the last minute to try to avoid too much storm damage.

Deadheading, including cutting down herbaceous tops, we keep postponing and often it doesn't happen until March and April. This is partly laziness, partly because we consider many of the dead heads add significantly to the scene (think of them covered with hoar frost), and partly because they may protect the plants in the winter. There are exceptions such as the flowered stems of hostas which we try to remove as soon as the flowers fade, and plants which might bloom a second time.

We inherited large numbers of snowdrops and daffodils and a fine clump of *Leucojum vernum* and *Colchicum.* We have spread hundreds of Leucojums and daffodils to different parts of the garden, and there is the problem of the dying leaves. Leucojums we find are perfect bulbs to associate with hostas particularly the early 'Thomas Hogg', and they also suit *Geranium macrorrhizum* which is not too tall in winter to hide the blooms. Leucojums and daffodils associate well with plants like *Geranium psilostemum, G. sylvaticum* and *G. pratense* which start into growth in May and soon cover the withering foliage, and daffodils are also tall enough to compete with the large evergreen *G.* 'Claridge Druce' and *G. endressii,* and ferns. They suit the large hostas, but there is a gap of about a month in May before the hosta leaves develop sufficiently to cover the not very beautiful daffodil leaves. Snowdrops we find do well in the lower drive where summer shade is so dense that grass does not grow.

As we have redesigned parts of the garden over the years we have had to do quite a lot of returfing of lawns and paths. I use an ordinary spade to remove turf from elsewhere and as I am not a particularly tidy worker the turves come in all shapes and sizes and often the cross-sections are more like wedges than rectangles. After they are laid and tucked into their neighbours as best they can, I rather brutally thump them into place with the back of my spade. There are many hollow places and little triangles devoid of turf, so I tear a turf apart with my hands, put the pieces in the required places and thump once more, and so on until the whole is reasonably even. I think this rough treatment is only possible in our light soil, and of course it often takes half the next summer before it all knits to look like a lawn, and it might have been easier if I had taken more care. It was quite hard work and my wife's heart used to sink when she heard the thumping going on, but the eventual result would have been no better and the work would have taken longer, so I mention it here because I have done some fairly large areas in this way very quickly.

The fire in our middle room consumes enormous amounts of wood but I have never needed a mechanical saw. Wood up to 6in thick I can easily deal with using an ordinary bow saw, keeping a sharp blade. Anything much over 6in thick has nearly always been the product of tree felling by contractors, and I require them to leave the pieces not much more than about 2ft long. However big the diameter I can deal with these quite easily using a set of steel wedges. The original wooden maul soon disintegrated and I have been using an ordinary 12lb hammer for the best part of 20 years on the same set without too much damage to the wedges – or me. We can burn logs in the house up to 3ft long and 6in in diameter, and shorter ones up to about 12in in diameter, although more often 12in logs would be split into two.

Living so close to the ground our attitude to wild animals is not sentimental and varies from awe for their capacity for survival to contempt for their proclivity to feeding and breeding to the exclusion of all else. For the most part the balance of nature seems to work well enough even in the unnatural environment of the garden and there are only a few that worry us. Moles I have managed to eliminate entirely, for the time being at least, and squirrels we suspect have occasionally spoilt the growing tips of spruce and silver firs. Rabbits are now a considerable worry. (In the past Mr Ovenden of the local rabbit clearing society kept them under control.) Foxes occasionally damage shrubs when chasing prey. On two occasions an animal made a systematic foray through our large beds of winter-flowering heathers causing some devastation which needed a growing season for recovery – it was almost certainly a fox. This year we have several foxes in the garden. One morning from our bedroom window I saw a rabbit walking from left to right past the gap in the low wall of the square, and a few seconds later I saw a fox walking from right to left. They must have passed each other amicably. Then more recently my wife from the bedroom window at about 4.30 a.m. saw a fox walking through the round arch into the square. It was followed by another fox, and she could hardly believe her eyes when yet a third fox (a younger one) followed the first two. They nosed about the square

66

for a minute or two, and, as we have usually found with foxes, in quite leisurely fashion made their way into other parts of the garden. Foxes never seem to be in a hurry, and unfortunately for us do not seem to be very keen on a rabbit diet. Bird damage has been confined to flower buds of early cherries, *Amelanchier laevis,* and sometimes other plants. You never know what they will fancy, and last year every single flower and leaf bud of an *Enkianthus campanulatus* 'Alba' which had never been harmed before was stripped.

My wife and I are untrained, that is we have never been taught the great garden crafts like budding, grafting, tieing back, earthing up, many of them concerned with growing vegetables and fruit. We are second to few in our admiration for a piece of real garden craftsmanship such as a fruit tree or rose superbly trained against a wall or a well kept kitchen garden, but our gardening is seldom of that type, although in different circumstances we could enjoy growing vegetables. Like most amateurs we learned from observation, by experience and reading. We started with one book of 350 pages, half of it pictures, which set out to teach us the entire subject, and I should like to pay tribute to all the 'stodgy manuals' as I have known them described on which the standard practice of gardening is so reliably founded. I hope therefore that no one will detect in these last two chapters any suggestion of an iconoclastic text book, but rather a conviction that some of our methods could be used with advantage elsewhere. We believe that anyone who is keen enough could have a garden of an acre or two with hardly any outside help. We are conscious that some of our ways are rather unorthodox and even unprofessional but at worst can claim that you will be unlikely to go far wrong if you adopt them. The omission of certain subjects does not necessarily indicate our disapproval; given time we would like to and hope to make more use of annuals to supplement perennials, propagate more of the medium-sized or small slightly tender shrubs, do better with climbers, have more small bulbs and 'Always go on learning'. I am one who believes that life is meant to be a struggle and that 'Man is born unto trouble as the sparks fly upward' and it is sure that if your main aim in life is to avoid both you should not choose serious gardening.

There is of course the question of the atomic bomb and other matters. Is it worth while starting any new enterprise which will take 20 years to mature, would we do it now? We have enjoyed making the garden, enjoyed watching it grow, and enjoyed looking forward to its full maturity; but would our enjoyment of the first two have been vitiated by the absence of the third? We don't know, only suspect that if we were younger and had to start in today's conditions we would do the same as before.

Think of the rewards, especially in our climate; November and most of December, so unpopular with some, but so often mellow; the severest of our weather not until January and February, but the sun is higher in the sky, winter will soon be over; then come the rigours of the English spring. I often think Browning must have been mad or perhaps homesick wanting to be in England in April when he was living in that most perfect of places, Florence, but in spite of all, what can be more exciting than the throbbing life, the all too rare sweet showers epitomised in Shakespeare's 'uncertain glory of an April day'?

Other Gardens

'Every garden has its own special and separate character, which arises partly from the tastes of the owner or his gardener, but still more from the situation, aspect, and soil of the garden. It is this that saves our gardens from monotony; if the conditions of every garden were the same, it is to be feared that the love of following the fashion of the day would make our gardens painfully alike. But this is prevented by the happy law that before success can be reached the nature of the garden must be studied, and the study soon leads to the conviction that we cannot take our neighbour's garden as the exact model for our own, but must be content to learn a little from one and a little from another, and then to adapt the lessons to our own garden in the way that our own experience (often very dearly bought) tells us is the best. And because of this special character in each separate garden it follows that each garden has something to teach, which cannot be taught so well elsewhere; and the happy result is that no one with a love for gardening who visits other gardens can ever go into a garden (especially if the owner of that garden is a true lover of flowers) without learning something.'

More than 50 years before Canon Ellacombe wrote that, the Lambardes or Randolphs were building the walls of our square, or so I like to think, as part of a well devised plan for a garden the like of which had not been seen here before. These walls still formed the centre of the Maxwells' garden as they do ours today, and determined the main aspect of all three. For the situation we have to go back to Sir John Howell and his predecessors, and as for the soil we can only thank God for it. This leaves the tastes of the owners to which, with respect to the Canon, I attribute most of the character of our garden. Many and varied are the things which help to make up people's tastes and in our case they certainly include other gardens and all that appertains to them.

Reflecting on what has influenced us I remembered a chart I bought in Florence showing the development of Florentine Art in the form of a family tree where full lines denoted a master-pupil relationship and dotted lines a less direct influence. The analogy is a good one I think; if applied to the making of our garden most of the lines would be dotted with a few solid lines denoting the direct incorporation of an idea or feature, or even an actual copy. The Hidcote concept of a series of relatively small formal garden 'rooms' connected by a 'corridor' as also in the later Sissinghurst undoubtedly earns a solid line. We have even gone so far as calling part of our garden 'Hidcote' where I am afraid for several reasons neither the design nor the execution has come off, but we have not given up and it is a nice challenge for the next year or two. One day standing on top of the steps above the Moat Walk at Sissinghurst I said that we must have a long straight path which can be viewed from above. We now have it from the tea terrace to the medlar; alas, the height is not there, and cannot be. Another direct copy followed one of the splendid garden parties at Wexham Springs my wife and I were invited to by the Cement and Concrete Association. Again it was a long straight path, the copy of which is now the path leading to the temple (not then thought of) which at that time had a considerable kink half way along which we immediately removed. I think a short path flanked by

From our bedroom window

dwarf conifers at Grayswood Hill gave us an idea which is realised in several places, one of which is the low planting of heathers in a direct line between the summer house and the Doulton urn. There are of course dozens of examples of plants, paving, ornaments etc which resulted directly from garden visits which would need solid lines and soon overcrowd my chart – but I am beginning to contradict myself. All the same if one had nothing better to do on a cold winter evening sitting by a good fire it would be an interesting exercise to construct just such a chart. As in most human enterprises it is most likely the sum of all the indirect influences, ie the dotted lines, which predominates. These influences may be material or fanciful, trivial or weighty, even sublime, of grandeur or simplicity, beauty or ugliness, principles or incidents, and are sometimes mere impressions, often subconscious. Apart from observation of the garden itself they can come from such things as talking with owners and gardeners, sitting contemplating in the garden or in the tea room or even car park, and looking at the countryside on the way home, and not least the tour of our own garden which invariably happens after a visit to another. Apart from specific visits to gardens there are walks, say, from Waterloo to Covent Garden through the Embankment Gardens not forgetting (ugh!) the South Bank. All five senses are involved to say nothing of the weather, time of the year and so on. In short all the factors which form the 'tastes of the owners'.

How fortunate we are in our part of the country to have within a car journey of an hour or so not only a number of the most famous English gardens open frequently but also dozens more open occasionally for the National Gardens Scheme, Gardeners' Sunday and other charities, and what better way can there be of spending an afternoon, or perhaps even better a morning or late afternoon? I have selected a few, all of which have some special appeal to us at the risk of disappointing some owners of the very many others we have enjoyed. Like Alice I will begin at the beginning with the two we visit most frequently but for the rest the order is pretty haphazard and certainly not in order of merit.

I start with Sissinghurst of which so much has been written that I hesitate to comment at all. We go there several times every year, admire the perfection of planting and maintenance, think it would be nice to see a few aberrations, deliberate or self-sown, realise they would not be in keeping, note that we have more trees, shrubs and views, are envious of the sheets of anemones, think it peters out a bit in the orchard in the summer, and then admire the splendid herb garden at the very end; in short a never failing source of inspiration for both of us.

Great Dixter we also visit frequently and have done so for many years, and Mr Lloyd's nursery has supplied many of our plants. In the past we have never been quite sure about his meadow garden. This year (1979) we have never seen Great Dixter looking better and we realise how the meadow and long border fit into the scene so well – but are still not convinced that the long grass suits the approach to the house. But who are we to say? Only that we could not emulate it here. But is some of our 'woodland' garden, provided we manage to acquire enough suitable self-sown seedlings, a close relation? Mr Lloyd is a great blaster of trumpets against the monstrous regiments of heathers and rhododendrons, and much as we like both in a way we agree with him; they are so often abused and are certainly not for every garden. Even if he liked them very much could he grow them in his soil? But we do not agree that heathers are only for massing in wide open spaces. We have them massed, in small groups, and even as individual plants, in different parts of the garden, where in our opinion they are both appropriate and attractive. Apart from the many features that are particularly associated with Great Dixter, we much admired the rose garden, cleverly sited not to be obtrusive in the winter.

On the way home from Scotland to Northamptonshire we visited Newby Hall both house and garden on a wet September day in 1965. In spite of the rain we enjoyed the well-designed formal parts with the long central vista full of interesting plants, and also the informal plantings of shrubs to the west of them. The owner had provided a numbered list of plants which we found helpful.

Wakehurst Place and Sheffield Park are on an entirely different scale. Those who know these gardens may be amused at our first visit. We had spent several hours at Sheffield Park and happening to pass Wakehurst on the way home thought we would just drop in to see if it was worth a visit. It was in Sir Henry Price's time and the suggested circuit was marked by a series of numbered stakes in the ground. When we had reached Number 6 we thought what a large garden we had seen; imagine our surprise on catching a glimpse a moment later of Number 60 on the return route! Both of these gardens have extensive collections of plants but are quite different in concept. Sheffield Park is a landscape garden of magnificent large trees bordering three large man-made lakes to be seen at its best in early summer, and again in October for its outstanding autumn colour. Away from the lakes are many more trees and shrubs mostly growing as specimens. It is the type of garden we visit say once a year for inspiration and information concerning ultimate size and habit of trees and large shrubs. Other landscape gardens which we visit for inspiration or would if they were nearer are Stourhead, perhaps the finest of all, Studely Royal with Fountains Abbey, and Blenheim Palace. It is interesting that all include extensive water, and my wife and I found it difficult to think of any to rank with them which did not. The reason could be that to get the required effect without water needs many acres of mown grass and, apart from the obvious difficulty of maintaining them before the days of lawn mowers, the people making such gardens could afford to have water and why settle for less?

Another type of large garden began to appear about 100 years ago, the rhododendron garden, of which one of the finest, Leonardslee, also comes into the landscape category. Fifteen years ago our reason for visiting these fairly often was easily accounted for as we were such enthusiastic planters. Today, somewhat chastened by droughts, but keen on the genus, we would go mainly to enjoy ourselves, and why not? Many of these gardens are in Devon and Cornwall and the west of Scotland; two nearer to us which we enjoy are the Valley Gardens at Windsor and Sandling Park, Hythe. The owners of such gardens were seldom very concerned with garden design.

In the *Journeys and Plant Introductions of George Forrest* there is a picture showing seed drying and below it 15 packing cases addressed to J. C. Williams, Esq, Caerhays Castle, Cornwall, England per T. Cook & Son, Rangoon, and I immediately thought of this when Dr and Mrs Knibbs whom we were staying with near Port Scatho one April in the early 1970s arranged for us all to visit Mr and Mrs Julian Williams and to see the garden. The Knibbs were our first tenants in the attic flat, and had made a very fine garden in a short time in Cornwall. Dr Knibbs used to give us rather tender plants which had not much chance in our climate – we sometimes wondered whether he was actually encouraging us, or pulling our legs. He was an Australian, and very cleverly grew many plants in Cornwall from his native country. We were shown round by Mr Williams and although it rained heavily for the whole two hours or so we hardly noticed it. We gazed in wonder at the profusion of the plants, huge magnolias, a superb *Michelia doltsopa* covered with blooms, *Magnolia nitida,* the original *camellia* 'J. C. Williams', to say nothing of the rhododendrons, and so much of it from those crates of seed. I remember Mr Williams' surprise when my wife named *R. bureavii.* It was a morning to put our little affairs into perspective.

Coming back to Wakehurst we are in a large plantsman's garden developed without a break by three successive owners since 1903 with a remarkable variety of well labelled plants of all kinds from 100ft trees to the smallest herbaceous plants, in a spacious and well-proportioned setting. Before 1965 it was the largest and most comprehensive private garden of the many we visited during our early 'plant education'. Since 1965 it has been leased to Kew by the National Trust, and it is marvellous to know that a garden of that calibre will continue to evolve at least as well as in the past. Something will be lost without the personal control of a private owner, as is already apparent in the uniformed attendants, the unfortunate institutional look of the house both inside and out, and the tarmac paths, but on balance these are perhaps small matters. Incidentally with the exception of Oxford and Cambridge Colleges and some of the older schools can one think of many institutions that do not look institutional? If someone replies 'Why shouldn't they?' I won't argue – it is a pity, but a small price to pay for democracy.

Grayswood Hill was a little too far for us to visit as often as we would have liked. In our early days we had never seen such a great variety of well grown trees and shrubs in a comparatively small area. It was also about the first private garden we came across with shrubs for sale and naturally we bought quite a few. We shall never forget a large *Magnolia x soulangiana* 'Alba Superba', in full bloom, against an evergreen background and a clear blue sky.

One summer day in 1957 near Brenchley we stopped to look at a magnificent half-timbered house. We peeped inside and could not resist stepping a few paces further through the wide open gates. We had never seen anything so striking in a garden, evergreen azaleas (probably amoenum), heathers, conifers against a background of trees and all in immaculate order. We saw on the pillar box that it was Brattles Grange, and took the first opportunity to visit it on an open day soon after. In two years we visited this garden six times, and we shall never forget talking to the owner, Mr Murdocke, in his early eighties, still planting camellias, and telling us how much better they were than rhododendrons. This was I think our model garden for a year or two, and it was here on our first visit that we saw for the first time *Viburnum plicatum* 'Mariesii', perfectly sited on a corner, *Cornus kousa,* and a spreading juniper. Mr Murdocke left soon afterwards and for some years now it has not been open to the public. We have recently discovered that the Lambardes at one time owned both Brattles Grange and Great Comp.

These were the great days of garden visiting for us, and they went on throughout the sixties, in fact until we became tied to our own garden by opening every Sunday, which unfortunately is the only day many of these private gardens are open. I will single out one memorable day about the end of that period. We were invited by Harry and Susan Smith to see their garden at Westcliff-on-Sea and two others in Essex. The Smiths' garden at a rough guess is not much more than one-eighth of an acre. Behind the house they have cleverly created an attractive vista with a fine lawn, summerhouse, small pond, beds of shrubs, and innumerable herbaceous plants and bulbs collected during their travels in this country and abroad. Our own front terraces and ruins owe much to 9 Merrilies Close, but we have a long way to go to equal Susan's planting. We then proceeded, all four of us, to Hyde Hall, Rettenden, where Mr and Mrs Robinson joined us and we went in convoy to White Barn House, Elmstead Market, where Mrs Beth Chatto, who had recently started her now well known nursery, was also making a three acre garden. Here too it was the profusion of plants particularly in the beds near the house that we enjoyed as well as Mrs Chatto's enthusiasm for extending into the then wild parts. It was a blazing hot day but Harry had not finished with us, so we went back to Hyde Hall where the Robinsons showed us their celebrated collection of roses, and also much more, the large collection of dwarf conifers, many trees and shrubs, and in the house the most attractive small conservatory we have ever seen. Round the large pond there was a vast number of plants many of which we had never seen before. By the time we got home at night we were half dead physically and might have been overwhelmed with envy or even jealousy of the things other people did better than we, but I can safely say we were not and never are, only thankful that there are still so many people with enough interest, ability and

Above: Taken in 1972 by Harry Smith in the doorway at the back with me. Susan is in front of us with Joy on her left. The girls from the Huis te Lande and some of the staff, including Dr Post the Principal, and Mr Wim Oudshoorn now the Vice Principal

Below: On the tea terrace one year before

drive for us to try to emulate; and there was always the thought if such things can be done in Essex which has even less rainfall than we do.

During a Scottish holiday in the early 1970s we visited Dunkeld to see the cathedral and old houses and noticed a garden open to the public that afternoon. I have forgotten if I ever knew the name of the house, but we liked everything about it so much we were almost tempted to wish we owned it. The garden sloped gently down to one of Britain's grandest rivers, the Tay, a few hundred yards to the east of the monumental masonry bridge taking the Perth–Inverness road over the river. All round are towering hills clothed with lush conifers, and the hills, house, river and bridge made a perfect setting for a garden in which we remember a considerable variety of plants. We wish this sort of opportunity to see a private garden on other than a Sunday happened more frequently, but we know why it does not.

Coming to 1979 and leaving out all the many private gardens we visited in the intervening years it is pleasant to think that we found a few new ones, that is, new to us. Warders, two acres in the middle of Tonbridge, full of plants, The Postern almost in Tonbridge we had been led to believe was a meticulously kept formal garden, which it is, but with such a wealth of well grown plants. Peter Godden's garden, Doghouse Farm, we had seen before, smaller, also with formal features and a fine collection of plants, and cleverly planned round the attractive house. This was in April and he was lamenting that the place was a shambles after the hard winter, no euphorbias, no hebes, nothing to see – if he had not told us we would never have noticed. Ilam at Hawkhurst has been made by Mr and Mrs Stapylton-Smith since 1973; we thought we would have a look one day when we were visiting the late Miss Davenport Jones's nursery almost next door (now so well run by Miss Strangman). How surprised and delighted we were to find not only a well designed garden but so many plants we had not seen before.

David McClintock gardens within a mile of us at Brackenhill, and has amassed a collection of plants which must be almost unique. We have referred to it as 'full of weeds without a weed in it', and were somewhat taken aback when a distinguished visitor to our own garden who had obviously misinterpreted that remark, looking at a rather unkempt patch of brambles, nettles, etc, said, 'David McClintock would like that'. Not at all. Both in the relatively wild parts where the plants mingle exuberantly and near the house where there are hundreds of small plants nearly all labelled in some way, David maintains it all under complete control, and you would have a job to find a nettle or a bramble, except some exotic varieties. The wilder part I think of as something between Christopher Lloyd's meadow and our woodland, and plants from Brackenhill already occupy their own little McClintockery here which we hope to extend in due course. Brackenhill is not open to the public.

There is so much more, summer evenings at Crittenden House with music and soft lights, music on the terrace at Beechmont before the Annual General Meeting of the Sevenoaks Music Club, superb views over the Weald, Glyndebourne, a miraculous *Clianthus puniceus* in a Cornish seaside garden which had never known more than 3°F of frost, Anglo-Italian style at Husheath Manor, and so it could go on, but I must leave room for something about the larger gardens.

At 61½ I can still get down to it. The purple and white flowers in the foreground are two varieties of the burning bush, *Dictamnus fraxinella*, plants which always arouse interest. Other herbaceous plants include *Potentilla* 'Flamenco' and *Achillea* 'Moonshine'

Above: The compact rhododendrons 'Blue Diamond' and 'Blue Tit' with heathers in April

Below: Evergreens and Japanese maples with *Berberis calliantha* on the right and the yellow *Cupressus macrocarpa* 'Goldcrest'

Above: Summer with *Cistus cyprius* in the centre and the fine blue *Picea pungens* 'Koster'

Below: Azaleas and rhododendrons in the front garden

I have known National Trust Gardens for longer than any others having been a member ever since I transferred from the Scottish National Trust which I joined just after the war. As well as those already mentioned we have enjoyed Bodnant with its wonderful dell so overwhelmingly luxuriant, the Powis terraces, trees, shrubs and picturesque ruins at Nymans, Tintinhull, small, formal in design, informal in planting, skilful use of colour, and so well suited to the XVIII century architecture of the house, Batemans, hardly a garden at all but how well the old house sits in it, and our publishers' garden at Stoneacre, where we so much admire the planting in the borders by the stone walls of the house, and the association of plants mingling together in small groups, such as hellebores with snowdrops on one winter day. How attractive the rough stone path looks leading from the gate up to the front door, and how uncomfortable to walk on, which illustrates one of our own problems, how to combine comfort and taste in paved areas. Our drive, forecourt, and the wide path leading to the stable are tarred but with three-eighths inch gravel on the surface, which we regard as satisfactory in appearance although not too pleasant to walk on, and the gravel tends to stick to one's shoes and find its way into the house and stable; but we think it is still preferable to smooth tarmac or asphalt. Our con-

The top terrace

crete slab paving is very comfortable to walk on, but we would not claim that it looks as good as the natural stone at Stoneacre and many other gardens. On the other hand we have seen gardens where the excessive use of natural stone looks affected and concrete would probably be better. Stoneacre, of course, has the added attraction of an interesting old house open to the public. We must not forget Mr Joy's trees and shrubs at Emmetts, and thereby hangs a cautionary tale.

We had known Emmetts before the garden unfortunately had to be separated from the house when it was first opened under the National Trust's control in

Above: Old brickwork and an old yew hedge

Below: Conifers and heathers, a patch of lithospermum and our original *Magnolia liliiflora* 'Nigra', from the forecourt with the large yew in the background

1966. Mr Joy, the Head Gardener, has been a regular visitor to Great Comp and as we had not been there for some years, one afternoon in 1979 on the way back from visiting a nursery we decided to call in and see him. Now one of our more eccentric habits is to have a collection of watches none of which has worked for years; on the odd occasion when we leave home and need to know the time we take our bedroom clock, small but rather heavy in my pocket, so we had little idea of the time although we might have guessed when we saw a builder's lorry leaving for the night as we approached the bottom gate. We drove up the long straight steep and very narrow drive to the entrance gate which was closed. I cannot remember if it was locked, but we stood for a few minutes and were pleased that it all looked even better than we remembered it, and then decided to cut our losses and come back another day. The bottom gate was several hundred yards away so instead of backing the car I decided to turn round and started the usual manoeuvres and in no time at all the car was at right angles across the road with a thick hedge in front and a high grass verge behind. It had been raining recently and we were stuck. Backwards and forwards a few inches we went, engine revving, wheels spinning on the grass, exhaust ploughing into the ground, and no apparent turning movement. We were desperate, not so much at our lack of progress, but for fear of attracting the attention of the occupants of the house just inside the gate. We became more and more hot and bothered, my wife trying to turn the front wheels, but at last as we edged round we came to a slightly more yielding part of the hedge, and after a few more goes we were away, leaving what I thought looked like devastation of Mr Joy's newly cut grass. We reached the bottom gate which to our renewed embarrassment was locked. We got the lady from the bungalow to open it, thank goodness she was at home, and we were off. It reminded us of a visit to another garden years before when we missed the way out and found ourselves on another estate road. We realised our mistake but, as often with me, stubbornly kept on saying there must be another way out until we ran through and broke an electric cattle fence across the road. Again we had the embarrassing business of knocking up the lady in the nearby lodge and informing her of our transgression.

We returned to Emmetts next day as ordinary garden visitors and have not enlightened Mr Joy from that day to this. We hope he did not blame the builders and that he will forgive us, the innocent victims of circumstance. After all that I must refer you for further particulars about National Trust properties to the Trust's own publications, and particularly Mr Thomas's recent book.

'Small is beautiful' is one of today's catch phrases written by a wise man and taken up by fools advocating back to nature and the like, that is to say no orchestras, no golf courses, and of course no large gardens. Would we feel safer if our defence depended on each maritime county providing its own Navy? Would the owner of a small private garden have been able to finance George Forrest? Still, I must admit that some of the large private gardens seem to have lost their identity, to use another current phrase, when they were extended beyond the original plan to accommodate the vast numbers of newly collected trees and shrubs that became available in the past hundred or so years, which tended to be planted as mere collections. Also the gardens thus became too big to be maintained under today's conditions with the consequent neglect not only of the extension but also of the original. Today with a few exceptions large gardens are owned by institutions which have often taken them over from the original private owners; two of the latest examples are Wakehurst Place and Hillier's Arboretum, and I think few people would have been happy to see the demise of such places, which was the possible alternative.

Certainly it is difficult for a large 'public' type garden to be a real garden which to most people must mean one closely associated with a house, and completely under the control of the owners, in fact one of the many things which combine to make a house a home – *pace* speculative builders' advertisements. It is difficult for them to avoid looking public, one immediately thinks of large notices containing the byelaws, litter bins, and they have offices and even laboratories and all the accoutrements necessary for the comfort of very large numbers of visitors. Such gardens have three main functions as I see it, botanical, to advance the scientific study of plants, horticultural, to encourage and advance the practice of gardening, and for the recreation of large numbers of people. When we are feeling a bit snooty we are sometimes inclined to dismiss the last of the three as more suited to public parks, but I think not; if we are honest we will admit that we visit not only for the second but also for the third, and if we had not seven acres of our own the last would be even more important. However, it is mainly for information about plants, that is size, shape, habit, scent, pruning etc, that we return to such gardens again and again, and only these large well funded gardens can hope to provide the necessary comprehensive systematic fully labelled collections today. There are the great botanic or similar gardens, Kew, Edinburgh, Cambridge, Wisley, Harlow Car and the Hillier Arboretum; the great specialist collections, Westonbirt, Winkworth, Kew Arboretum and Bedgebury; gardens of the Royal Parks, Savill, Valley, Hampton Court, Regent's Park and St James's Park, and the better public parks like the Victoria Park, Bath, Harrogate and not only the most fashionable. I remember being surprised at the interesting plants in a public park in Slough. All these we have visited, some once, some many times. They are mostly so well known that I need not say any more here, and of course there are many more that we have not yet visited.

Ruins and similar places where the garden if it exists is only secondary have always attracted us, as already exemplified by the Forum in Rome. In 1956 we were astonished to see the ruins at Villers-la-Ville near Waterloo, and there are countless others in this country like Melrose Abbey, Bayham Abbey near here, Kirby Hall, the Welsh castles, etc. Ought ruins to be tidy with mown grass or not? is a question on which we have no very strong views, but I think we lean towards tidiness. I have always had a feeling for the memorials to great people, and one recently especially so. It was on a bitterly cold February day when we were returning from one of Ivan Sutton's string quartet weekends at the Brudenell Hotel at Aldeburgh. We saw from the road Boulge Church which looks as if it is in a field, on the edge of a wood, and we eventually found our way along a track to it, and there in this very isolated churchyard we stood above the flat granite slab which covers the tomb of Edward Fitzgerald, the translator of Omar Khayyam. The rose bush was raised at Kew from seed brought from the poet's grave in Persia. Very different was the time we visited the large private cemetery at Stoke Poges after paying our respects to Thomas Gray in the churchyard. It was a warm summer day and we were hardly prepared for such a large cemetery with so many individual memorial gardens, many of them very small, and so well planted and looked after. All such experiences have, I feel sure, influenced us here.

If one visits a famous nursery expecting to find mature specimens of all the plants in the catalogue well labelled and attractively displayed in a garden setting, one will almost certainly be disappointed. Even if it was possible in the past no commercial nursery can afford such luxury under today's conditions, and in any case the need is surely catered for in the other gardens I have been writing about in this chapter. Nurserymen have enough to do supplying plants especially for those like us who want the less common ones. It was probably different in the great days but the only nursery I remember that could claim to include a garden in its own right was Sunningdale, although woodland nurseries like Reuthe's rhododendron wood at Crown Point near here would nearly qualify, and of course Hillier's.

Nevertheless for over twenty years our idea of a perfect day out is a trip to a nursery familiar or new to us, nearly always in the country and well off the main road. We take our lunch or tea in the car and find a nice quiet place with a view or in a wood to eat it. If you take the B2110 out of East Grinstead, leave it just before the sharp bend at the railway bridges and carry on along this road for a few hundred yards you will come to an obscure country lane on the left. Go along it and you will be in the Gravetye estate, where one day we walked a little way up one of the forest rides having just eaten our lunch and noted a large conifer with an iron label beside it marked W.R. and the date of planting. Drive along the lane through the wood, always forking left for nearly a mile and you will reach a lane which will bring you as it has brought us almost every year for twenty years to Ingwersen's Nursery. It is now owned by the firm but was originally leased to Mr. Will Ingwersen's father by William Robinson himself. You will never find it difficult to acquire a box full of plants to take home.

Fairseat Nursery near us is approached along an unmade road leading to a piggery near which we found the entrance which looked as if it hadn't been used for years. The last owner, Mr Fielden, who has recently died, used to produce one of those skittish catalogues peculiar to certain one-man nurseries. We discovered some years ago that he lived in the same London hotel as Mr Moulton-Barrett's stepmother. When we last went there we literally could hardly see any plants for weeds. There was no one there but we saw a small collection of plants ready for despatch, so we hung around and fairly soon an old friend of Mr Fielden's turned up who told us the stock had been left to him and he was gradually disposing of it. We came away with a number of bargains.

We often take the car and tour around our local Kentish lanes nearly always on the way to some objective such as a house, garden, church or perhaps the coast or some Dickens haunt, sometimes not going further away than half a dozen miles – a one-inch Ordnance map adds greatly to the fun. If you want to try this after visiting our garden, turn left into Comp Lane as you leave and keep to the 'top' road past Crouch to Gover Hill (good view), wend your way to West Peckham church (a nice detour along a little cul-de-sac). West Peckham (called on the map on page 127 Little Peckham) is hardly a village, but it has most of the requirements – a shop, a pub, cricket on the green and one of the most interesting churches in the district. The early XIVth century chapel at the

Map showing boundaries of Platt and Offham
parishes today and the area of the original Comp
transferred from Leybourne to Offham in 1934

*Based on the 1975 Ordnance Survey 1:25,000 map with
the permission of the Controller of Her Majesty's
Stationery Office, Crown copyright reserved*

83

east end of the north aisle was, in the XVIIth century, converted to a charming family pew for the owners of Oxen Hoath, the descendants of Nicholas Miller the Elder who sold land to Sir John Howell of Great Comp in 1606. Among the tablets on the wall is one to Sir Nicholas Miller, his grandson, who died in 1658. Continue past Yotes Court noticing ahead of you the spire of another remarkable church, a copy of that of St Martin-in-the-Fields. Mereworth Church was rebuilt in 1744/46 by the Earl of Westmorland of Mereworth Castle. Turn right into the Seven Mile Lane, B2016, cross the main A26 and take the first left, a narrow lane up to the redundant church of East Peckham, miles from East Peckham, and usually locked, but the view across to the 170ft high Hadlow Tower is extensive. Carry on between the grounds of Roydon Hall and Mereworth Castle, passing an old carriage entrance to the latter, wend your way down turning right at the foot into Nettlestead Lane with views of the Medway Valley and Nettlestead Church and you will eventually find, on the left, the lane leading to the Rock Farm Garden Centre.

Our friend, Sue Corfe, has a delightful garden which she opened to the public for the first time last year, and an interesting garden centre. If it is only to buy plants Mrs Corfe will be very glad to see you from Wednesdays to Sundays, and you certainly do not need to go by the roundabout route I have described.

Here we have a relatively modern phenomenon, the nursery/garden centre attached to an attractive garden open to the public. In a small way we do this ourselves and would be more than happy if more other owners did. Well known ones we have visited include Great Dixter, Farall, Treasure's of Tenbury, Wisley and White Barn House (Beth Chatto).

The ultramodern large garden centre on a main road must be one of our poor old country's few growth industries and many old established nurseries have had to follow the trend to survive. If I say rather condescendingly they fill a need it must not be assumed that our needs are never supplied by these places – we have bought many plants from them.

Before leaving the subject of nurseries I must just mention the pleasant lunchtime walks from my former office to Vincent Square for the Royal Horticultural Society's Shows which used to take place every fortnight throughout the year, and of course Chelsea Show itself. I used to particularly enjoy the spring shows, the flowers and foliage brought on just a week or so early, the scents pervading everything; it was sometimes difficult to settle in the office that afternoon thinking of the long time until Saturday when I could compare our progress with what I had seen. And, as on all public occasions, one enjoys the people as much as the exhibits. My first acquaintance with hundreds of plants was at Vincent Square either on nurserymen's stands or in the competitions. Hillier's remarkable exhibits deserve a special mention. On one occasion I saw, I feel sure, over 100 varieties of holly.

Finally a couple of quotations to sum up how infinite are the possibilities of gardening: Harry Smith used to quote one of the Rothschilds starting a lecture, 'It will I think be generally agreed that no garden however small should have less than two acres of rough woodland', and, 'It is impossible to visit a garden however small and however uninterested the owner without learning something.' The second quotation is in fact from J. T. Cameron with a slight bow in the direction of C. Northcote Parkinson.

84

Books we find useful

Dost thou think, because thou art virtuous, there
shall be no more cakes and ale. . .

In the last chapter I considered some of the things which I believe have helped
to form our gardening tastes, but there are others and less obvious, for surely
one's tastes in everything must be reflected in such an all-embracing subject.
One of my favourite books is *The Concise Oxford Dictionary of Quotations*.
What makes a quotation or a tune memorable is something which cannot be explained and is one of life's mysteries. The above is one of my favourites from
Shakespeare; the slow movements of any of Beethoven's last five string quartets
would supply some of my favourite tunes, which does not mean I do not like
'Lili Marlene' or 'A stitch in time saves nine'. I have been tempted to write at
length on this, but I think two turn-of-the-century preferences and a few aver-
sions will suffice. Neither Richard Strauss nor Rudyard Kipling can put a foot
wrong with me; my wife would agree about the former, but would have reserva-
tions about the latter. For what passes for architecture and music today (except
Shostakovich) and for things like advertisers' English, the modern Church of
England service and its literature, gimmicks, band wagons and fashion in
general we have little sympathy, but at the same time would not wish to do the
impossible and put the clock back and would not wish to live in a different time
from our own.

I have always enjoyed food, with very few strong dislikes, and I actually like
milk puddings, and have done so all my life. But it took me to the age of 61 to
learn from a newspaper comment of a director of a whisky firm that it is not
sacrilege to add some water to his product. I tried the small dilution he recommended, and I must reluctantly agree that it brings out the flavour.

Being rather serious about what we try to do we both need to watch out in
case we become pompous, so I hasten to add that we both liked the two old men
in Eric Barker's 'Just Fancy', Jimmy Edwards as Mr Glum in 'Take It From
Here' and Frank Muir and Denis Norden in 'My Word'.

At a preliminary meeting in connection with a Fruiterers' Company function
in the garden I explained to Mr M. R. Barton, the Master, and the Learned
Clerk, Mr David Hohnen, at rather great length what facilities we had to offer,
and finally back in the forecourt I proudly pointed out the car park. I think I
took the point when Mr Hohnen asked if I wore a uniform, but I doubt if I will
ever learn.

I hope I have some sense of humour. The type of true story I find funny is
when the late Field Marshal Slim, asked by a photographer to smile, replied, 'I
am smiling'. I have even invented a riddle about the garden which poor as it
may be is my own and I am quite pleased with it. What is the difference between
Cameron and some modern architects?, the solution to which you will find if
you need it in the next chapter.

But enough of this. I hope I have made my point and I will now go on to consider some gardening books and writers. We are not great collectors of books
and have only a modest couple of shelves of those directly concerned with

gardening. These I like to think of as a fairly select little library including some that are, so to speak, indispensable. Of those in the category of reference books the one most often used by us is Hillier's *Manual of Trees and Shrubs*. It contains adequate and botanically accurate descriptions of over 8,000 woody plants hardy in this country, and includes much more of interest concerning choice of plants, cultivation, names and so on. If it can be said of any book that it should be in the possession of every gardener who wants to grow trees and shrubs this is it. Mind you, it can be a little overwhelming to find 117 different oaks taking up eight pages and 83 different varieties of Lawson's cypress. One feels one would like to grow the lot which is quite unnecessary except in places like Kew or Hillier's own arboretum near Winchester; even if one had the space many of the varieties are not sufficiently different from each other. Which to select is one of the great gardening problems; it is what this chapter and the previous one are partly about, and it is hardly too much to say that few serious visits to gardens would be complete for us without this book either in our hand or more often in the car, or to be consulted on our return home.

We have the 1951 edition of *Trees and Shrubs Hardy in the British Isles* by W. J. Bean who was for a time Curator at Kew. It is a mine of information on all aspects of the subject historical, botanical and good cultivation. A new, much enlarged edition has recently been published in four volumes, but for our purposes the one we have got hardly needs updating. In our edition he is rather scanty on garden varieties (cultivars) but this information we can find elsewhere, for example Hillier's manual which at the risk of oversimplification may be regarded as a companion volume with shortened descriptions to the standard authority, Bean.

View from near the entrance to the garden. Note three design features – the focal points (Chilstone sundial and Doulton urn), the straight path and the curved path disappearing in the distance

Perennial Garden Plants by G. S. Thomas which is a much larger version of his *The Modern Florilegium* which was the catalogue of the Sunningdale Nurseries and much used by us in the sixties is the equivalent of Hillier for herbaceous plants. The original, smaller version, in its few pages, did more to influence the garden at Great Comp than almost anything else, but don't think it is always quite so easy as Mr Thomas says (or said then) – just as well perhaps.

Ingwersen's *Manual of Alpine Plants* we bought last year. Although we do not grow many of the very small alpine plants the book includes also small herbaceous plants and we would not like to be without it.

These books cover most categories of plants except bulbs. I am glad to say we have plants in our garden not mentioned in any of them but they are very few. We do not have any great urge to keep completely up to date with all the latest plant introductions and are content to get such information from the press, magazines, gardeners and gardening visits.

William Robinson's *English Flower Garden* we have in the 1906 edition. It is more than a reference book, the first part being a treatise on the subject in the forthright style of the man and the day. In the second half, which is an alphabetically listed description of trees, shrubs and flowering plants of all kinds, we have occasionally found a plant not included in any of the modern references but still obtainable. This monumental book is a pleasure to handle and well worth seeking out.

Two books of a more general nature are *Twentieth Century Gardening* by Charles Eley and *The Well-Tempered Garden* by Christopher Lloyd. I like Mr Eley's style but my wife finds it a bit heavy going. Here is the start of his chapter on gardening books:

'I beseech you that next after the Scriptures you study that great volume, the works and created objects of God, strenuously and before all books, which should only be regarded as commentaries'

FRANCIS BACON: Epistolae 6.

It is quite certain that, of all men, Bacon did not undervalue the use of books, and the fate of Tomlinson of Berkeley Square is an additional and more recent warning to any gardening aspirants who, conscious of difficulties, may put excessive faith in aid from books.

Gardening books are legion, but in the multitude of these counsellors there is no complete safety: the reason for this reversal of biblical teaching is not always the fault of the books. Any failings must be shared in varying proportions between the readers and the books.

It is well-nigh impossible for a writer of a technical book, even if he be a successful and experienced teacher, to anticipate every doubt or difficulty that the book may create for his readers. It has been said that 'reading is thinking with someone else's head instead of one's own' and therein lies the crux of the matter.

Mr Eley's book contains just about all anyone would need to know to make a not too time-consuming garden of mainly trees and shrubs, and I made constant use of his advice particularly during the early days when we had to choose so many of our plants. A garden designed on his principles would be rather limited in scope for us because of the lack of herbaceous plants, but I feel sure that for many people today with an acre or two of ground it could well be the ideal. If you wanted to find out how to make it more interesting the first stage might be to read *Plants for Ground Cover* by G. S. Thomas in which he includes shrubs as well as herbaceous plants. It was fascinating to make a pilgrimage a few years ago with the Horticultural Club to Mr Eley's garden at East Bergholt, and to see so many of his trees, shrubs and views with which I had become familiar from the pictures in his book.

If as an exercise in whimsy I were to ask an imaginary Mr Greenfinger to read these books and then design a garden would he produce a splendid hybrid or would he retire in confusion saying the cross was impossible, so different were the authors? Mr Lloyd's book is more than half as long again as Mr Eley's and includes much of interest on trees and shrubs, but he is not a tree and shrub man in the usual meaning of that phrase. Most of the book is packed with information on just about all other aspects of plant cultivation and planting including, as he terms it, fruit and vegetable specialities, evidently all based on his own direct experience, and with no concessions to labour-saving for itself. You are left in no doubt about his likes and dislikes which leads to the answer to my question, which is that the splendour or otherwise of the garden would depend on Mr Greenfinger himself; my advice to all would-be gardeners who are interested in plants is to read both books and go and do likewise.

Of the books mentioned so far, only in *The English Flower Garden* is there anything about garden design, and I suspect for every book written on that subject there are dozens on plants and cultivation. Our own reading on design has been mainly in books such as *The Shell Gardens Book,* but we recently bought Percy Cane's *The Creative Art of Garden Design* which is very well illustrated with gardens he has designed. His liking for stone terraces and paving would be too expensive for most clients today, and it is fortunate that in our opinion at least as good an effect can be obtained with concrete slabs.

Michael Haworth-Booth is another stimulating writer. One does not have to agree with all his views. *Effective Flowering Shrubs* aims to show how a garden can be colourful throughout the growing season by the use of shrubs alone, and also labour-saving by means of what he calls close boskage. He has much of interest to say about soils, garden climate and other cultural matters. It was from him we learnt the folly of digging-in fallen leaves, nearly as bad as burning them – they should be used as mulch.

Yet another was A. T. Johnson who with his wife and not much other help made a garden in North Wales which he describes in *A Woodland Garden*.

I am very glad to possess Gertrude Jekyll's *Home and Garden, Wood and Garden* and *Colour Schemes for the Flower Garden.* These books are about gardening of another age, almost another world, reminiscent of some of the early photographs we have of Great Comp. In the introduction to *Colour Schemes* Miss Jekyll starts, 'To plant and maintain a flower border, with a good scheme for colour, is by no means the easy thing that is commonly supposed. I believe that the only way in which it can be made successful is to devote certain borders to certain times of year; each border or garden region should be bright from one to three months.' This is the very opposite of our idea. I expect that it required a lot of attention from a number of gardeners to keep each of the seasonal borders in the state of perfection she no doubt demanded which went so far as to condemn goldfish in the Gold Garden; 'their colour is quite wrong'. But there is much that is still valuable for today in these books which are well illustrated with photographs and well written in the style so evocative of that more self-confident time. Of the specialist books I will only mention *Modern Rhododendrons* by E. H. M. and P. A. Cox which was so essential to us in the early days when we were selecting from over 1,000 species and hybrids from Messrs Reuthe's remarkable nursery. Incidentally we once tried to visit their own nursery at Glendoick, and failed to find the entrance.

We have the 1973 *Pocket Guide to Heather Gardening* by Geoffrey Yates, which apart from cultural and other information contains the most complete descriptive list of those plants, and I believe has been reprinted fairly recently.

A useful Heather Society publication is *A Guide to the Naming of Plants* by David McClintock. It would be of great assistance to anyone looking for an introduction to the subject.

There is an altogether different type of book of which I have not read as many as I should, and that is the lives and journeys of the great plant collectors either written by themselves or others. When in 1950 I began to travel along the South Lambeth Road, usually in a No 88 bus on my way to my office, I was much intrigued to see a side road which had the curious name Tradescant Road and repeated itself after about 100 yards. Years later when my office was at Lambeth Bridge I went into the churchyard of the Parish Church of St Mary's and was surprised to see two fairly large tombs, one of Captain Bligh of the *Bounty* and the other of John Tradescant, father and son, gardeners to Robert Cecil, 1st Earl of Salisbury, and to King Charles I, botanists, plant collectors, etc, and the real founders of the Ashmolean Museum, the first public museum in Britain. Tradescant Road was constructed in 1880 on the site of the Tradescant house called the Ark, one of the sights of London. It was sold with four acres 14 perches for £16,150 just three years after William Elsdon, builder, paid £375 as part of a larger deal for one-fifth acre on which stands 55 Cavendish Road. Land in Lambeth was apparently worth twice as much as land in Clapham. Still later after I had retired we went to look at the tombs and were surprised and not very pleased to see the church boarded up and looking quite derelict. But there is a happier sequel and some of our garden entry money for 1980 is earmarked for the Tradescant Trust which has been formed recently to ensure the future of the building and churchyard as a museum, garden and conference centre. John Tradescant the Elder married Elizabeth Day in 1607 (in Meopham Parish Church near here) and John the Younger was baptised there in the following year. I could enjoy writing more about the remarkable father and son, but must instead refer you to Mea Allen's *The Tradescants*. Miss Allen lives in Walberswick which is commemorated in the name of another road in Lambeth off Tradescant Road.

These are only a few of the books from our collection, and just think of the hundreds more that have been written, many of them no doubt just as important as the ones we have mentioned.

For example a book I have only just read is *Living Tradition in the Garden* by Richard Gorer, in which he discusses forthrightly many aspects of design and cultivation, most of which we heartily agree with, and much of which we had already put into practice here. For many gardens the note about the plant he refers to as *Geranium collinum* and which I think is now called *Geranium procurrens* should be transferred from his chapter on Ground Cover to his chapter on Plants to Avoid, unless you like creeping buttercup. He even has the temerity to criticise the fashionable one-colour garden as seen at Hidcote and Sissinghurst. It depends on what you want, of course, but we agree with Mr Gorer that such gardens are something like furniture stores where 'one passes from the Regency Dining Room to the modern Swedish Lounge'. To us after the initial impact they tend to be boring. Some of his topics, eg 'florists' flowers, are of no practical value to us, but should not be ignored by anyone interested as we all should be in garden history. I was amused to find George Forrest who from his photograph looks like the archetypal lowland Scot, described (no doubt by the printer) as 'Georges'.

Of the many magazine articles we have read the one in the October 1970 issue of the Royal Horticultural Society's Journal (now *The Garden*) by Brig. C. E. Lucas Phillips on the design and control of small gardens should be read by anyone starting a garden and not necessarily just a small one. Incidentally the pictures are by Harry Smith. We have also learnt much from articles in the press, and particularly admire Mr Fred Whitsey's weekly article in the *Daily Telegraph*. His style is unlike any other, his asides often as informative as his main argument. He has the rare ability of combining the basic information needed by us all at one time or another during our gardening careers with an unending flow of new ideas and variants of the old. We wonder how he finds time to try out all these things and to look after his own garden.

Finally there are books about gardens open to the public, and we never cease to wonder why so many of the same public buy none of them but rely on the press or a notice they happen to see. We are seldom without *Historic Houses, Castles and Gardens* on any trip we make beyond our own county boundary.

I have already quoted at length from *In A Gloucestershire Garden* by H. N. Ellacombe 1822–1916. His father the Rev H. T. Ellacombe 1790–1885 was vicar of Bitton near Bristol from 1835–50 having been trained as an engineer. In that year he was succeeded by his son who had been his curate for two years. The vicarage garden was notable in the father's time and became even more celebrated in the son's who was there for 68 years. The 126 years life span of father and son strikes one as quite extraordinary, and yet my own grandfather was born in 1823 and my father died in 1951 – 128 years. Incidentally, my old church, the Rankin Church in Strathaven, was built in 1843, about the same time as our present church here in Platt. The first Minister from 1843–1899 was the Rev Alexander Rankin and the second from 1899–1945 was the Rev T. M. Dey, 102 years, which also beats the Ellacombes. Canon Ellacombe's book has been described by Mr Eley as '. . . suggestive not only of gardening but above all of charm and refinement of a kind that is typically English' and the sort of book to put you in the right frame of mind, an appropriate sentiment with which to end this chapter.

Opening to the Public and Visitors

A question that irritates me whenever I hear it or see it written is, 'Do you like *people* or *things*?' It is not meaningless, of course, and both Joy and I would, if we were compelled to be categorised, admit to an inclination to things including of course plants, and I suppose there are collectors so obsessed with that pursuit that they develop a positive distaste for people. For me the question has little meaning as I regard things of all kinds as the great backcloth and setting of human activity and the better things as necessary for the better life. Think of a great cathedral empty: is it more impressive when full of tourists or when it is the setting of a great religious service? Why should the enjoyment of beautiful surroundings to whatever event one happens to be attending, in theatre, concert hall, cricket field, church, or even drawing room, be considered incompatible with, to use one of my least liked modern words, 'caring'? We both agree that a garden is like a house and wants to be lived in, and a big garden like ours even more so. Some of my most memorable experiences have been in the presence of vast crowds, state occasions in London, football matches in Hampden Park (I have been there on the terraces with nearly 150,000 other people), Test matches, the Open Golf Championship; yet when I contemplate the human race in the lump, or even democracy and the steady march to mediocrity with which it appears to be concomitant, I am more inclined to agree with the sentiments of Dean Swift who principally hated and detested 'that animal called man; although I heartily love John, Peter, Thomas and so forth'.

On the whole, we like to think of garden visiting as very much a personal matter even although we also feel our garden is enhanced by the presence on a fine day of a hundred or two hundred people, and we are very sorry when exceptionally only a dozen or two people are there to enjoy it. Anyway I have no hesitation in saying we like opening to the public. It started in 1966 when friends from Lancashire, a county which does not include many gardens among its attractions for visitors, wrote, without telling us, to the organisers of two charities suggesting that we should be included. Although we were prepared to open and did so for a local charity on the evenings of 19th and 20th July 1967 when we took our first money ever from the public (108 shillings), we did not think we were ready for the national schemes, but the following year we agreed and our first open day was Saturday 1st June 1968 for an entrance fee of 2/- (10p). It was raining hard that afternoon. Not a soul came until the rain stopped at about five o'clock and almost immediately a number of cars arrived and we were in business. The next day, Whit Sunday, brought us over 200 visitors, seldom exceeded today. For two years we opened for the Whitsun and August Bank Holiday weekends, then we tried Saturdays and Sundays from May to October, then Fridays and Sundays, then for a year Wednesdays and Sundays and now back to Fridays and Sundays.

The snags have not been many and certainly have been outweighed by the rewards for two very ordinary people receiving visitors from all over the world. Obviously supplying tea, taking entrance money and selling plants make extra work and are also a tie which we are particularly conscious of on a fine day when numbers happen to be unsatisfactory, otherwise the snags relate only to garden damage and litter. I am glad to say both have up till now been negligible; however one Friday recently I was boasting of this to some visitors who were just leaving when, almost as I was speaking, someone was removing about two thirds of a rare fern we had bought a year before, kindly smoothing the soil so we should not know – the remaining one third disappeared a few weeks later. Of course, some cuttings *are* taken, occasionally rather stupidly from a prominent position, but we have not been much aware of it. Near the end of the 1978 season I was standing at the garden entrance when suddenly I saw the Doulton urn in the actual process of falling off its pedestal. A child aged about six with her parents almost beside her had climbed up to see what was inside it. The middle part was broken into two pieces which I was fortunately able to join with Araldite. We are not insured against damage to our ornaments, as I am sure the premiums would be very high. In fact there was nothing in the urn but soil, too often the case with our ornaments, as this type of gardening is by no means one of our stronger points.

When we started in 1968 I stood at the front door and the cars were parked in the forecourt, but by 1970 we decided that the remainder of the front field (which had occasionally already been used for that purpose) should be a car park for up to 60 cars, and we started hunting for a suitable kiosk, eventually buying a nice little summer-house from Knight's of Reigate, which I surrounded with paving and low retaining walls and erected one of the four pairs of iron gates which had come from the old rose garden. The men who delivered the summer-house erected it on my levelled site, and within an hour of their departure we were sitting in it, furnished and with a carpet on the floor, having our lunch. This summer-house has been one of our most useful acquisitions in its dual role as well as providing a focal point for one of our vistas. I also incorporated into the paved area a small bay on which we place the plants for sale on open days. On the occasions, mainly in May and early June, when we have a

The drive, with 'Stonehenge' and the car park entrance on the left

92

good number in the garden and they are in the buying mood for plants, and perhaps the car park is getting a bit congested, it can be quite hectic on one's own because in addition to the actual transactions the plants have to be discussed, departing visitors have comments and often wish to talk about plants in the garden. On very busy days Joy spends quite a lot of time running backwards and forwards between the tea room and the summer-house in case she is needed. We like it when we are as busy as this.

On that very first Whit Sunday hours before opening time a tall well weathered man and his wife arrived at our front door saying they were particularly interested in gardens and plants and would we mind etc . . . My wife, seeing his tripod and wanting a photograph of our first spectacular young *Viburnum* 'Lanarth', asked him if he would kindly take it and send us a copy. When it arrived by post a few days later whose name should appear on the letter heading but Harry Smith, Gardening Photographer. Harry and Susan were two of the most assiduous garden visitors, who must have been to and photographed about every possible garden in the United Kingdom and many abroad. Susan called herself the plumber's mate; Harry took the pictures and Susan could always produce the names. From then until Harry's death in 1974 they were two of our most frequent visitors and we shall always be grateful for their encouragement of our early efforts. We had seen many pictures of our garden taken by other people, but Harry was the first to show us what professional horticultural photography at its best could make of it. He was one of the characters we can ill afford to lose and we are sad that he cannot come and take photographs today. He would have liked our ornaments. An event always associated with the Smiths is the annual visit in May of second-year students from the Dutch girls' horticultural college, Huis te Lande, Rijswijk. For several years Harry had arranged an itinerary including many gardens in the south of England, and he accompanied the group. They have been coming here since 1971. This year (1980) Mr Wim Oudshoorn showed us a report on our garden which one of last year's girls had prepared. Although she had enjoyed the garden for many of what we like to think of as the 'right' reasons, she obviously was not very keen on the design, ornaments, paving etc., and much preferred Sheffield Park. We are of course genuinely flattered when we are seriously considered with such a world-famous place, but it seemed to us an odd comparison. Much as we like Sheffield Park it is on such a vast scale and is so lacking in small intimate corners that to us it is on the verge of not being a garden at all, but a pleasure ground for want of a better name. When I have been cutting the grass for about an hour amongst the trees and shrubs and abundant ground cover what a remarkable change it is to arrive at the ruins, where masonry and small 'rock garden' types of plant predominate. But it was an interesting report and one of the benefits of opening one's garden to the public is occasionally genuinely to 'see oursels as others see us'.

It is my practice on open days to do some weeding right up until I see the first visitors which often might be as late as 12 noon by the time they get to, say, the temple, with Joy holding the fort at the entrance. One Friday I was working in front near the top when I became aware of two men and a boy forcing their way through some prickly berberis and rose bushes from the car park. Shortly afterwards Joy heard two rather disgruntled women walking through the proper entrance saying *they* were not going in that way. What had happened was that the party had arrived rather early, one husband had bought tickets and had been told by Joy that the best way round the garden was to go up to the top first and so on. He had gone back to the car, collected together his party, proceeded to the top of the car park and started to force his way through the boundary shrubs, but had obviously not convinced the ladies. Afterwards we compared notes and I discovered that Joy was (a) slightly puzzled because the women had taken so long to arrive and (b) very puzzled at the complete disappearance of the men. I think peace was declared.

We have no stories to match that, and really open days are not to be treated with levity, but there are many funny little incidents, a few of which are worth relating. We used to provide set teas for parties, as often as not for clubs with a lot of elderly members, many of whom came only for the bus run and the tea and whose first questions on arrival were invariably 'Where are the toilets?' and 'Where is the tea?'. One day a particularly large party of between 60 and 70 managed to find their way through the wrong door just half a minute before we were completely ready and at our posts to supervise their seating, which we always did. One of the tables was a picnic bench of the type which looks like a capital A with the cross-piece extended on each side to support a bench seat and with a slatted table on top. The balance is delicate and certainly could not contend with two well built ladies sitting on one side simultaneously and no one on the other. Hence two ladies and set teas for six became mixed up on the floor: not at all funny at the time.

Many of our visitors' comments are made to the tea helpers, Joy included, who is often told, 'It's a lovely garden, isn't it?' Other questions range from 'Is this their dining room?', 'Is this the kitchen?' to (to Mrs Packman) 'Are you Mrs Cameron's cook?', to which, to save further questions, she answers, 'Yes'. Most people realise who we are so it is quite funny when sometimes they don't and ask, 'How many gardeners have they?', 'Can you tell me who owns this place?', 'Can you tell me the name of this place?', 'Does anyone live in the house?'. And the occasion when a young man with a small family party having spent some time in the forecourt taking a good look at the house walked up to Joy and said, 'Does some Lord live here?'

When, as I sometimes do, I address a coach party from the steps by the sundial I usually mention at the end where I come from in Scotland. My wife says, 'Don't say that. It has nothing to do with the garden', but it is certain if I don't that it will be the first question I am asked privately afterwards, so I will say something about it here at rather greater length than I usually do, and starting, strangely enough, in the Kent County Archives office. We were looking for information about the Lambardes, who owned Great Comp for many years, when I found a beautiful scroll written in 1906 by R. H. Owen Thomas with the pedigree showing the descent of William Gore Lambarde, of Bradbourne Hall, Kent, from King Alfred. It was of no value in tracing the Lambardes as it reverted to the female line when it reached his grandmother Harriet Elizabeth Naesmyth. However, on looking back another five generations I was astonished to find in the direct line none other than Anne, the Duchess of Hamilton, of my home town Strathaven. It took me right back to our little golf course one afternoon in the middle 1930s. It was during my holidays when four visitors arrived

Above: Heathers and conifers in September. *Cotinus coggygria* 'Notcutt's Variety' and the dwarf spruce *Picea mariana* 'Nana' in the foreground

Below: One of the best of all shrubs for autumn colour, *Cotinus americanus,* with the tower behind

Erica vagans 'Valerie Proudley', *Polygonum* 'Donald Lowndes' beside an upright juniper

Genista hispanica and *Ajuga reptans* 'Purpurea'

Deciduous and evergreen planting with the perfect cone of *Picea albertiana* 'Conica'

The bright patch of *Lithospermum* 'Heavenly Blue', in this mixed planting near the large yew

and wanted caddies, unfortunately not available at Strathaven, so my father and I carried the clubs for the two ladies, Madame Paravicini, the wife of the Swiss Ambassador, and her daughter. From memory I think the two gentlemen were General Poore, the Duchess of Hamilton's brother, and the Marquess of Douglas and Clydesdale, who flew over Mount Everest and later became the 14th Duke of Hamilton and Brandon and Scotland's premier peer. I remember to this day the daughter singing a little golfing song to the tune of 'The Girl I Left Behind Me'. In the song the singer's ball went into a bunker and 'from there to the green I took seventeen, and then by God I sunk her'. The event added a little excitement to our rather mundane but pleasant enough existence. The party had come from the Grouse Lodge about six miles south of Strathaven in moorland country, and known to history mainly as the destination of Rudolph Hess in 1941. He failed by only a few miles and landed in the next parish, the Strathaven Observer Corps Post having plotted the course of his Messerschmitt. It was called Dungavel and there was a small, private airfield. In the 1930s aeroplanes were still objects to be looked up at in the sky, and whenever we saw one in Strathaven it was likely as not piloted by the Marquess as he was invariably called. Another of his interests was boxing, and one of the absurd stories we used to be told as boys was that the family moved to the Grouse Lodge from Hamilton Palace which was demolished (in my time) because his parents wanted to remove him from the company of the young local toughs, his boxing friends. I believe Hamilton Palace, which must have been a wonderful place in its setting near the river Clyde and where Chopin once stayed, was demolished because of the effects of coal mining on the building and its surroundings.

The Duchess Anne, who was born in Whitehall Palace, was the daughter of the 1st Duke of Hamilton, friend of Charles I, and executed shortly after him in 1649. His title went to his brother William Hamilton, Earl of Lanerick (Lanark), and on his death by a patent of 1643 the dukedom devolved on her. By Cromwell's Act of Grace in 1654 the Hamilton estates were confiscated and the Duchess Anne had to leave Hamilton Palace. She occasionally resided in Strathaven Castle and is reported to have fired on Government troops as they passed through the town. She died in 1716, after which Strathaven Castle fell rapidly into decay.

Strathaven is a pleasant town of about 5,000 people 17 miles south of Glasgow. It is the country of Scott's 'Old Mortality' which is centred on Tillietudlem or Craignethan Castle, the ruins of which are in attractive country about eight miles east and worth a visit (Strathaven Castle though smaller is believed to have been embellished by the same architect, Sir James Hamilton of Fynnart, early in the XVI century.) John Graham of Claverhouse, later Bonnie Dundee, passed through Strathaven in 1679 on the way to Drumclog where his troops were defeated by the Covenanters and an inn in Strathaven demolished in the present century was known locally as Claverhouse. In the old churchyard are the tombstones of William Paterson and John Barrie, shot in 1685 in Strathaven Castle by Captain Ingels and Bloody Bell, and William Dingwall shot at the battle of Drumclog on Sunday, 1st June 1679, by Bloody Graham of Claverhouse. In modern times Strathaven was the retirement home of Sir Harry Lauder until his death in 1950.

Above: Azaleas in the front garden

Below: *Sedum* 'Autumn Joy', *Anaphalis triplinervis,* and *Polygonum amplexicaule* 'Atrosanguineum'

To confirm the tombstone inscriptions I telephoned an old colleague from my days in the Lanarkshire County Road Surveyor's office, Mr William Fleming Downie, who told me he had just had a history of Strathaven published, and I was pleased to buy a copy. Strathaven had its share of 'characters', some of whom I remember vaguely in my youth, and one of Mr Downie's stories in his excellent book amused me to the extent that I will repeat it here. It concerns one called Old Caulkie, who lived in Ballgreen, and porridge. Now porridge, a subject which is really too serious to treat flippantly, is essentially a fluid but according to my maternal grandfather should, as it comes to the boil, go 'plop-plop-plop', and not 'sizzle-sizzle-sizzle'. It is made from oatmeal, salt and water, and can be eaten for breakfast in many ways, of which two would be satisfactory for me. First, and preferably with cold top of the milk, or, as my uncle in Strathpeffer used to have it, with a large bowl of cold milk beside it, each spoonful of porridge being dipped into the milk. To be avoided at all costs are warm milk, sugar and syrup. However, Old Caulkie's method is new to me, and I quote, 'Another of his delicacies was porridge which he made once a week and poured it into a drawer in his dresser. Each day he cut a slice of porridge from the drawer, heated it over the fire, and had it for breakfast.'

My father had come south from Strathpeffer in Ross-shire where his parents, who had been forced to leave their ancestral country in Strathconon, farmed a croft at a place called Gower at the foot of a hill known as Knockfarrel on land given by the Countess of Cromartie. I think my liking for 'estates' was much fostered during school holidays spent there. My father learnt his golf on the Strathpeffer course in the days when special trains ran from London direct to the Spa. The crofters' life, though simple, was not primitive as all the men and some of the women did part-time jobs as well. Mr Ellis was a railway signalman, my Uncle Finlay was employed in the pump room where my Aunt May was a masseuse, and my Aunt Mary ran a delightful tea room for spa visitors in the chalet near the top of Knockfarrel and one of *the* places to visit.

My wife comes from Geddington, one of the Northamptonshire limestone villages so different from those in Kent, which has the best of the three remaining Eleanor Crosses and a mediaeval bridge across the Ise Brook which rises fifteen miles away near the battlefield of Naseby. She had been previously brought up on a 300-acre farm at nearby Pipewell, so like me she was used to plenty of open space, but her father died when she was only ten. He is buried in the churchyard at Rockingham, the village nearly taken over by Corby, but still one of the most attractive in the country, dominated by the castle and church on the high ground to the south.

However, I must return to the subject of opening arrangements for visitors. We do not like notices such as PRIVATE if they can be avoided and we prefer to have the outside double front door open; so we need to be on the alert as occasionally a large family party has walked straight into the house, opening the inside front door in the process.

On a different note, one day last year a man arrived with his wife and he made some sarcastic remark about paying 50 pence, which provoked me into telling him that if we charged what it was worth it would be £1. He followed his wife into the garden in some dudgeon, saying, 'And you'd be bankrupt.' An hour or so later, on leaving, he came right into the summer-house and said to me, 'I want to humbly apologise.' Apparently he felt he had been cheated previously, as the last garden he had visited was not as good as his own little patch.

Our ruins, although not meant to deceive, have created great interest and caused some speculation, the most informed type of question suggesting they might be old fragments recently repaired. I was rather amused when one rather know-all type, after airing his views on the architecture of our house at some length, asked quite seriously if there had been a monastery connected with the site at one time. For those who have not solved my riddle of the last chapter this is a suitable place to say that I build ruins while some modern architects ruin buildings.

I used to think that some of our great novelists introduced more coincidences than could possibly happen in real life, in *Oliver Twist,* for example. Enough have occurred here in our rather short history to vindicate Dickens in my eyes, in fact to demonstrate the old adage of truth being stranger than fiction. Many concern people who knew people in my or my wife's villages, know people we know, or used to play hockey here about 60 years ago but had no idea this was the place until they arrived and vaguely recognised it, and so on. I think three examples are worth recording.

One of the few arguments I have had over the admission of a dog was with a gentleman from Essex who turned out to be a veterinary surgeon who had recently come south after 14 years' practice in Strathaven. He had been at school in Rutherglen with Bertie Couperthwaite and at the vet college in Glasgow with Willie Munro, two of my old golfing mates.

In 1971 my wife and I decided to take part in a garden tour with the Heather Society which included a visit to Sir Frank and Lady Morgan's garden near Amersham. This was on a Saturday and the very next day one of the groups of visitors to Great Comp left a very heavily-built man in their parked car as he found walking difficult. We were pleased when his friends returned a short time afterwards and said he really must see some of the garden, which he did. On his return he made a remark to the effect that surely with all this work we could never go away, which I refuted by mentioning our visit the day before to a garden at Amersham. He asked whose garden, and when I told him he said he was Sir Frank Morgan's sergeant in the HAC in 1914. We were so intrigued that we wrote to Sir Frank, and in his reply he said he was amused because the last place where he would have expected to find his old friend Bill Bailey was in a garden. They had known each other since 4th August 1914 when, on joining 'A' Battery HAC, Sir Frank was posted to his sub-section. They went through the whole of the war, had never lost touch over all the intervening years, were both over 80, and both have since died.

A few years ago Mrs Denison, from Platt, said her mother-in-law from Jersey was coming to stay, and she would bring her to see the garden the following Sunday. They duly came and Joy made a point of speaking to Mrs Denison senior as she was about to leave. Detecting a Scottish accent, and finding she came from near Glasgow, Joy said, 'Don't say Straven?' Mrs Denison is now over 80, and not only did she come from Strathaven but her parents lived in the next house to my mother's parents, and therefore she grew up with my mother and aunts and uncles. I went into the house and was able to produce, from a collection of old photographs, a picture of the lady (then Miss Jean Riddell) in her graduation robes of Glasgow University. As a matter of interest her sister Chrissie, who used to fit me with shoes, married my old English teacher, John Brown.

We enjoy our conversations at the gate whether the subject be house or garden, serious or frivolous, and we are often ourselves the beneficiaries. There was the gentleman from Vancouver who told us to look out for coloured seedlings of *Acer* 'Prinz Handjery'. We have transplanted several with encouraging results. We are presented with plants which admittedly is sometimes just a nuisance, but how nice to have *Viola* 'Maggie Mott' given by a garden visitor who on leaving introduced himself as the head gardener from Chartwell, Mr Vincent. Just before one of our concerts when I had much else to think about a visitor gave me a sealed envelope containing some seeds. Mr Schofield had acquired a single seed of *Silene armenia* over 30 years ago by chance in a packet of seeds of *Silene caramanica* which he had selected from one of the annual RHS lists, all of which failed except that one seed. Seed from this plant had travelled with him from Cheshire through Derbyshire, Bedfordshire and, finally, Kent, and he hoped it would give us as much pleasure as it had given him. I think it probably has.

On one occasion last year the help was not only highly practical but almost providential. A family from Holland arrived one morning on a non-open day, said they were in the trade, and duly walked around, and asked if they could camp in the car park. Later in the afternoon the husband came down and offered to do some pruning as he was at a loose end. Now it happened that only the previous day a branch of our neighbour's large oak beyond the temple had fallen into our garden, the largest I have ever been faced with, and it was not completely severed, but poised rather dangerously. I had cleared some of it and was really quite worried about tackling the rest. Our Dutch friend having produced a very small pruning saw from the car was soon happily working away, and all was well a couple of hours later.

In all our 12 years of dealing with the public, incidents of the other kind, unpleasant or awkward, have been few. Whether that is a tribute to us or the gardening public is not for us to judge, but it makes us happy to look forward to the next 12 years.

Occasionally, usually after some building work, my clothes are so dusty that I am not allowed beyond the garden room without stripping off my outer garments. Such a day was one of those raw, very misty early afternoons in January 1973 when I was sitting on a box in the garden room eating my 'piece' (ie sandwich, to non-Scots) – I think I had been using a wire brush, one of those circular ones you attach to an electric drill I had hired for the job, to remove whitewash from the inside stable walls. There was a knock at the back door and a large gentleman announced, 'I am H. Newell Dodge from San Francisco, and this is my wife, and this is my son.' He said he was trying to trace his ancestors and had been referred to us by the Maidstone Museum via the Rector of Wrotham in connection with Dodge's Charity. My wife was out shopping, no fires were lit, what was I to do, banished from the house as I was? Well, to cut a long story short, I sent them round the garden which they were unable to photograph because of the mist. Thankfully my wife returned just afterwards, hastily lit the lounge hall fire, produced what documents we had, and made tea while they perused them. They had a great feeling for their past and were delighted that we had kept the charity going. Four years later on a beautiful hot sunny open day Mr and Mrs Dodge arrived once more and they were highly pleased to see the old place so full of life with 150 visitors in the garden.

As soon as it becomes known that there is a fairly large garden open to the public, organisers of functions are attracted like bees to a honey pot. We welcome functions, both our own and other people's, whether for charity or not, but have now reached the stage when we have so many activities of our own that we can seldom consider accepting other bookings. My wife was a keen member of the Women's Institute and one of our early social events was an evening barbecue complete with a barrel of beer; other WI events have included two county garden parties in 1968, the Platt WI party to mark the golden jubilee of the WI in England and Wales, and various garden meetings.

We have had art exhibitions, Scottish dancing, wedding receptions (including the arrival of one young couple by helicopter), and important functions and meetings arranged by the Chipstead Lake Cheshire Home, Friends of Walthamstow Hall School (Mini-Glyndebourne), The Fruiterers' Company (Mr M. R. Barton of Platt was the Master that year), Malling Rotary Club, Heather Society, National Trust Weald Centre, Church of England (Social Work), and perhaps our swan song in this direction, a flower festival in aid of Platt Church Restoration Fund arranged by Mrs Marie Vinson and her daughter Mrs Julia Cooper.

Apart from the helicopter we have had visits from a steam traction engine, glider, No 42 London Transport double-decker from Headcorn, so highly polished you could see your face in it, a 1914 Clement-Bayard, and Rolls-Royces of various vintages.

We cannot recall if the fact that our stable had 80 seats (see Chapter 12) had anything to do with the idea behind an 80th birthday celebration for Miss Ethel Breething, first chairman of the Sevenoaks Music Club, but on 27th June 1975 it duly took place. She had been asked to wear a long dress and be ready to be picked up, and thanks to some careful staff work had no idea of anything else until not long before Mrs Florentine Immink's car turned into the drive. Few who were there will forget the expression on Florentine's face as she drove down into the forecourt, horn blowing, hand waving excitedly to the assembled guests. The concert in the stable was given by some of her closest musical friends and was followed by a supper party.

We first met Mr Tom Wright of Wye College when he was writing his book in the Gardens of Britain series and that is how Great Comp came to be associated with a course he was arranging on the Management of Large Gardens. The members were to arrive here at about five o'clock on the 16th September 1978, and go round the garden, Joy was to arrange supper followed by lectures in the stable by the Curator of Villandry, Comte Marc D'Estienne D'Orves, and Professor Rene Pechere, President ICOMIS IFLA (1977). We knew it was an important course, but were hardly prepared for a list of participants including 40-odd owners, agents, head gardeners etc from some of the best known houses and gardens in the country. Without exception all pre-arranged events at Great Comp whether highly important or less so, individual visits or coach parties, small or large, gardening or concerts, public or private, are preceded by worry on the part of the Camerons about everything, but particularly something we can do nothing about, namely the weather. It always has been and always will be; so our excitement can easily be imagined as five o'clock approached with hardly a cloud in the sky and the shadows perfect. As so often happens in this life we were soon brought down to earth by a telephone call from Mr Wright to say they were still at Sissinghurst. By the time they arrived and I said my little piece on the forecourt steps it was still a fine evening and all went well, but of course an hour or so late. Half-way through the supper I went into the yard for some reason and noticed three people (whom I assumed were course members feeling the heat) sitting on the stone seat by the boy warriors, but towards the end I suddenly remembered to my horror that last week during David McClintock's lecture I had invited anyone interested to come and hear the Villandry lecture for which they could pay £1, and there they were sitting in the yard. I dashed out to apologise, and found Sir Cyril and Lady Pickard and Mrs Malcolm Brooke enjoying (or so they said and I almost believe they meant it) the sight of the moon completely obscured by the earth's shadow (which I had known about but had forgotten). If you want to empty a room quickly I can think of few better ways than to hammer on a table and announce there is a total eclipse of the moon. The course duly reassembled in the stable including our three friends, from whom I did not even try to extract £1, and Mrs Brooke sat down upstairs. The lights were dimmed and someone groped his way to the seat beside her. It was Lord Digby with whom she and her late husband, Bill Meyrick-Hughes, had been closely associated many years before, and whose parents had been very kind to them during a difficult period.

After all that the serious business of the evening proceeded until about half past eleven which brought to a conclusion what Tom in a note to us called a memorable evening.

There are many things which combine to make our concerts the rather unique occasions which with due modesty we believe them to be, and one of them is the arrival of the audience up to an hour before the concert to walk round the garden; and one of our own pleasures is to see them from the house as they arrive, in due course to reappear in various parts of the garden, particularly the ladies in long dresses.

Floodlighting parts of the garden started with our concerts and for a year or two extended to both sides of the house, but is now confined to the front. I always like to think it is a pleasant sight to see the lights as one comes in to the bar at the interval, and I hope some of our audiences walking up the lower drive on their way home see what I mean when I talk about our Westminster Abbey.

Living in an Old House

If our thoughts turn to the origins of Great Comp we have to go back at least to Saxon times, the name being derived according to Hasted from a Saxon word meaning camp or fortification but more likely to mean field. We have no documentary evidence about the building before the present century, but it is certain that an archaeological survey of the land for about 50 yards round the house would reveal fascinating remains of foundations, drains, paths and refuse dumps. We have come across all these, our finds over the years having been mainly in the front and incidental to digging for garden development. We found a lot of pottery fragments which were identified at the Maidstone Museum as probably XIth century Continental, and of course it is always interesting to find out what sort of dinner services were used by more recent owners! We have been told that Comp Lane used to be much nearer to the house, and when digging a trench for a water pipe and altering the adjacent shrub beds during the winter of 1978/79 I found a bed of stones about 10ft wide which could well be the remains of an old road but not, I think, Comp Lane. In 1970 when I was making the steps up from the forecourt to the front lawn I found that the existing dwarf dry stone wall was laid on a substantial brick foundation parallel to the house. As I have also found remains of foundations at right-angles to the house in line with the northeast gable there is some evidence of building between the present house and Comp Lane, or were they garden walls?

The main house dates from about the early XVIIth century with many subsequent additions including a Victorian porch, an extension to the southwest end which we call the cottage, and outbuildings. Recent repairs in the cellar have revealed further evidence of two interesting projects. It looks as if the house was extended to the northeast and a new chimney erected probably in the XVIIth century and then much later that a new chimney breast in the drawing room was built out to make it symmetrical in the end wall of the room. Apparently it was also at this time that nearly all the stone windows in the southeast elevation were removed and replaced with wood because there is an interesting stack of mullions, transoms etc, in the cellar which supports part of the extension to the chimney breast, or were they unused stone sections intended for an extension which was never built? But why stack them there? – probably just as a dump, but we may live to find out more about it and perhaps even salvage them for use elsewhere. In 1975 we extended the drawing room to a length of 30ft which involved demolishing part of the southeast terrace and rebuilding it. The retaining wall I built for the new terrace is at least the third, as I found the remains of a wall between the previous one and the house. For many years we had been puzzled about an archway just above ground level in the northeast elevation. It apparently was an access to the cellar which had been filled in to ground level. Recently I removed the infilling and found a small tunnel which is now a useful entrance to the cellar which will enable us to make better use of it as a store for garden materials. These few examples may be enough to show some of the interest of living in a house that has been in continuous occupation and evolution for some centuries. Following the death in 1955 of Mrs

Heron Maxwell who had come to live here with her husband in 1903 planning permission was obtained for conversion into three separate dwellings. As early as September 1956 we employed Mr G. B. A. Williams, an architect recommended by Mrs Dance of the Society for the Preservation of Ancient Buildings, to prepare a detailed survey of the existing house, and subsequently to obtain byelaw approval for the conversions. The main part of the house was to be for ourselves, the attic converted into a self-contained flat, and the southwest ex-

Great Comp May 1957. Note hawthorn hedge now removed

tension into a cottage. Having obtained the approvals we then, over a period of a few years, employed builders directly, with us doing most of the decoration ourselves; I seem to recall that we used 3cwt of that still admirable material Walpamur distemper which is so difficult to get today. We have found nothing like it for covering old walls. These three conversions cost so little at the time that we dare not mention the figures.

On the whole we have been well served by builders and I hope it is not invidious to mention only three who have worked with us for many years. Mr W. Paul of West Wickham worked for us at 55 Cavendish Road, continued to maintain it for us after we left, converted the attic and cottage here, and did much of the repairs to the outbuildings until he retired. Since then we have been equally fortunate in finding Mr R. Baldwin who lives only a few hundred yards away. In addition to maintaining the house he has been prepared to work with me on any repairs and alterations. Mr Froud, our electrican, comes and has half finished the work almost before we know he is about.

During the Maxwells' time the outside was hardly altered, although we have seen drawings of a most ambitious scheme. They built the middle chimney, bricked up one of the windows in the middle room and also added a fourth dormer window for the southwestern attic bedroom. Internally they 'improved' the three main rooms by altering all the fireplaces including a completely new central chimney where there had never been one, and panelling the dining room, the middle room and the staircase hall with old and good reproduction oak. The panelling and the middle room fireplace we like, but the other two fireplaces were not to our taste and we have replaced both. As a matter of interest we were hoping to find an old inglenook, but were disappointed, and eventually decided to extend the dining room by blocking up the existing flue and using the adjacent flue of the kitchen range.

I think it was Michael Haworth-Booth in one of his gardening books who was rather scathing about old houses, mentioning things like damp, draughts, dry rot, woodworm and leaking roofs, all of which we have experienced except the first, and all of which we have overcome at least to our satisfaction. We have no central heating, only a few night storage electric heaters including one of six kilowatts in the dining room. In general the one in the dining room is the only one we use, and then only when the outside day temperature is under 40°F. We are seldom cold which is partly due to the good sense of the early builders in giving the house a southerly aspect. During the coldest weather we make a very large wood fire in the middle room which after a couple of hours can be uncomfortably hot. No longer do we wonder how they kept warm in the country in the Middle Ages when the population was so much smaller and timber and cheap labour were so plentiful. This fire heats the chimney breast in the small spare bedroom above and we therefore move into that bedroom when appropriate.

There are of course other troubles connected with living in an old house in the country such as mice, rats, squirrels, birds, insects, spiders, fallen leaves in gutters, poor water pressure due to old pipes, dust from behind the panelling or between the floorboards. These too we have either overcome or learned to live with.

Several times we have been aware of a loud buzzing down the dining room chimney, and we now know that it is most probably a reconnaissance party of bees. Usually they go elsewhere, but on two occasions they have succeeded in establishing a hive in the house. The first time was in the flat roof over part of our own bedroom, and we were warned of the possibility of honey dripping into the room. However, nothing much materialised, and they must have died during the winter. The other was in an attic bedroom chimney. Our tenant lit a fire to try to smoke them out, and you can imagine his surprise when the wax melted and the whole hive descended into the grate. Fortunately he still had beside him the piece of hardboard which had blocked the opening, and he hastily slapped it back, where it is to this day.

Jackdaws deserve a special mention. Our first chimney sweep was asked to clear all the disused bedroom chimneys which had been blocked presumably by jackdaws. He could hardly get his rods through, but eventually came downstairs with four sacks full of debris. So far so good. That same summer Joy's sister came to stay and every morning for at least a week she brought down enough sticks to light a fire. Apparently jackdaws drop twigs down the chimney by the hundred until enough become wedged to provide a foundation for their nest. Three times since we came here a jackdaw has fallen down the drawing room chimney from a nest in an adjacent flue, which is a very expensive way of having the chimney swept; a thin film of soot covers the whole room. In spite of the fact that the bird has flown about the room from window to window for several hours, no china has ever been broken. The last one was actually in January 1980 and it was about the last straw as the room had just been specially well cleaned. We must do something about it, and the next time we have a builder who doesn't mind heights we will have the chimneys wired in some way.

There are also features which would hardly come into the desirable category of estate agents' advertisements nor presumably of the man in the Clapham omnibus, which I positively like. These include stairs, corridors, passages, odd corners (ie wasted space), small window panes, moulded doors, windows and skirting boards (except in the kitchen and bathroom), open fireplaces throughout, many external excrescences consisting of bits and pieces added on during several centuries up to 1979 *et seq,* and a generous supply of outbuildings, in other words almost typical of the rambling rectory so unloved by the Church of England today. It may seem strange to some, but my wife shares my feelings even if the housework is made a little more onerous. What is certain is that we make use of all these features either in a practical way or by just enjoying the fact that they are there, and during the whole of our time we have gradually brought most of the space into use as stores, garden sheds, garden shelters, tea room, concert room (converted stable), sitting alcoves, etcetera.

We have had some disappointments such as a mounting block which we thought might be masonry but which turned out to be rendered brickwork disintegrated by ivy and not worth keeping. We also wonder sometimes if we have committed some acts of vandalism, of which three possibles come to mind. There were two valve wcs with rather splendid mahogany seats which we replaced with modern appliances and I am afraid destroyed. A very large dresser in the old kitchen we mutilated by cutting into two halves and destroying one half; the other half we still use. And then there was the detached outside lavatory complete with a three-holer (two adults, one child) which is now a very nice summer-house. The only major external alterations in our time were the rebuilding of the second bathroom, and the extension to the drawing room, both on the southeast elevation, which had already been subject to several excrescences. Both could be considered and in fact proved to be controversial, but we are certainly satisfied that they are a distinct improvement in appearance on what existed at the time. Surely we are right to regard Great Comp as our home and not a museum, and in these circumstances there will often need to be some concessions to modern methods and materials.

To sum up we enjoy living there at all times, even in the severest weather, and manage to do it very economically, and in due course hope to leave it rather better than we found it. There is even considerable satisfaction in actually spending money on repairs such as in the cellar which we need not have done at all, as it would have lasted long enough for our time, but in this case we did carry out the work in 1979 which we had kept putting off for 22 years. For a few hundred pounds, no more than the 1957 estimate, we believe we have made it good for another three centuries. To cure a slight penetration of water in wet winters we intend to concrete part of the floor next winter after which we will have a splendid cellar over 70ft long with cathedral-like windows set in 4ft thick walls, and a fine vaulted passage, which will be useful as well as attractive.

Staircase and door leading to terrace   The Lion summerhouse

Referring back to Michael Haworth-Booth's remarks I must point out that we have always been prepared to use the rents and even some of the garden entrance money for repairs and improvements. I would like to warn anyone with a hankering for such a place to think twice if most of their life has been spent in towns, if they are not prepared to have tenants, and if their only income is or will soon be a pension from their employment. And all this, of course, is quite apart from the matter of the garden.

In spite of the crude arrangements in the early days, many friends and relations came to see us either for the day or to stay for a night or two, and one of our most welcome visitors was George Stone from Toronto. He was the fiancé of June Plant, one of three Canadian girls who had descended on us like a whirlwind one stormy winter evening in 1954 as our first tenants after we had furnished the basement at 55 Cavendish Road. George arrived at 55 one evening just as a vacuum cleaner salesman had started to demonstrate. For some extraordinary reason George sat on the sofa without removing his hat or raincoat, looking like Philip Marlowe, and watched; I can see him now. We had a perfectly good vacuum cleaner, and told the man, but he assured us that we would be surprised how much dust he would collect from our carpet using his model. He went through all the usual patter, finished his demonstration, and then with a great flourish emptied the container on the floor; his was the surprise, in fact he was nonplussed, not a thimbleful of dust. Strangely enough we still bought his machine to leave behind at Cavendish Road, and brought our own with us here.

George was going to Austria but had brought a full set of golf clubs and wanted to sample our famous courses including St Andrews, so we said if he didn't mind the inconvenience he could make his headquarters first at Cavendish Road, and then here. He had several spells here and did some very useful weeding of the ash paths in the square, removing many barrowfuls. One of his life's ambitions was to spend a night alone in an old country house. His chance duly arrived on the 25th April 1957 when Joy and I had to spend the night in London. There were no lights, no access to the attic rooms, little furniture, about 14 rooms, to say nothing of corridors, cupboards, etc., a howling gale, torrential rain, thunder and lightning all night, and George. He was mightily pleased to see us back next morning, and I see from the diary that we spent the next few days decorating two bedrooms in one of which he slept in a camp bed – those were the days! A few years ago he returned with June and their son Geoffrey under more normal conditions.

One Sunday night shortly after George's escapade we were sitting in the dining room having lit the fire after a day's gardening. Before going to bed we decided to have a last blaze and threw on a rather large old basket we had found. The resulting blaze was very much more than we had bargained for, and it set the chimney on fire in spite of it having been swept just before we moved in. A large open chimney on fire is not something I recommend to the faint-hearted. Large lumps of red-hot soot descended and propelled themselves well into the room. The heat was so great that we could not get near; all we could do was to shovel up the lumps and deposit them on the terrace. After an hour or so we managed to get near enough to put the hose pipe up the chimney and as the worst seemed to be over we started cleaning up the room. However, I thought I would go outside to have a look, which again had us worried as there was evidence of a considerable fire near the top with a rather frightening display of flames and sparks blowing towards the Oasts. There were now no stairs to the attic, and as we had no ladder we were unable to see what was happening up there, so in spite of it being a Sunday night we at last decided to call the Fire Brigade. Just before midnight Joy lifted the receiver of our old-fashioned manual exchange party line which took so long to respond that she kept tickling the instrument to hasten the process. This of course attracted the other member of the party line who had gone to bed, and having been told of the trouble by Joy spent half the night worrying if our house had been burnt down. After what seemed ages but was no doubt only a minute or two Joy managed to get through. Now, at that time the only person in either Platt or Borough Green we knew was our grocer, Mr Cloke, of the Borough Green Stores, so it seems almost inevitable for this sort of story that ten minutes later the Borough Green Fire Engine arrived in the charge of the same Mr Cloke. The first thing they asked for we couldn't supply, a dustbin, so they used our best brass coal bucket. They were in marvellously good spirits for that time of the week, and soon satisfied themselves and us that everything was under control – and so to bed.

We had let our furnished flats in London chiefly to Canadians and Australians and have kept in touch with many of them ever since. Jean Shaw, one of the three (the other was Pauline Mackenzie), has been back several times including last October. In 1958 we welcomed her brother Bill who bought a bicycle in July from a shop in Paddock Wood and sold it back to them in October before he left for home, having toured this country and the Continent, chiefly visiting battlefields. In June 1973 we were honoured to have a visit from their father Mr James R. Shaw, the Regimental Sergeant-Major in the Second World War of the 48th Highlanders of Canada. He had joined the same regiment when he was 17 in the First World War and was awarded the Military Medal. He died in 1974 and we were very pleased that we had been able to show him over Chartwell and Batemans, as he had been a great admirer of Winston Churchill and Rudyard Kipling.

Throughout our married life the style of such entertaining as we had done was doubtless influenced by the relatively spacious drawing room of 55 Cavendish Road with its 12ft 8in ceiling, and no less the setting of the public rooms here (a strange Scottish expression but no worse than reception rooms). They were fine for entertaining friends and relations with young children at Christmas and for the occasional 'estate' party. Our liking for a modicum of ceremonial is pandered to by the progression from the drawing room through the middle room with its roaring fire to the dining room and back again afterwards, and reached its climacteric with a large party during our first Festival (I use the word also in its other meaning of crisis).

Bernard King's recital was to be followed by supper in the house for 80 people, obviously no room for processions. The 15th September 1973 was one of these very warm sultry days I seem so fond of, but as soon as Bernard started to play we heard a few faint rumblings of distant thunder, and just as he reached the slow movement of the Appassionata Sonata, thunder, lightning and torrential rain of an intensity I had only experienced before in Southern Italy, at one point completely drowned the music. He played on as if nothing was wrong and of course there were many comments later on the appropriateness of the piece; how Beethoven would have loved it; someone even suggested that the storm improved the last movement. We reached the interval, and I got up to give a few instructions about the supper arrangements. When I had finished the Bishop of Rochester, who had been in seat No 1 in the front row, said to me, 'Now, Mr Cameron, tell me about the stable'. I had scarcely opened my mouth when the lights failed, the last we saw of them for more than 12 hours, and we were to have a lecture with slides by Harry Smith the following afternoon. Our candles were not as conveniently placed as they should have been. To Joy's horror she found that some well meaning helpers had decided to prepare for the supper by setting a match to the two big wood fires which, of course, were intended to be lit immediately before supper, and would be burnt out by then. This was our crisis. We decided there and then to have supper during the interval and, unbelievable as it seems, the rain nearly stopped for long enough to get the guests into the house. Candles had appeared from various sources and with the roaring fires and that marvellous spirit of cameraderie which always asserts itself on such occasions Great Comp has seldom seen as convivial a party. One little incident put things in perspective for me; this was when I was anxiously

111

pushing my way through the crowd to see if everyone was fed, and I overheard Peter Cousins and Michael James calmly discussing the state of the building industry. Other little incidents included the flooded yard which Iris Wilson traversed after removing her shoes and stockings, the water backing up from the drain in the stable to the consternation of at least one member of the audience, and the Watsons' floodlight. Long before the Festival we had been on the scrounge for floodlights, and the late Dick Watson, a local friend, had said that he had several mobile gas floodlights used in his business and would be pleased to lend them. I think he must have forgotten about it, but just before the Festival his son Brian travelled more than 50 miles each way to get them for us. By then we did not need them, but said they would be useful in an emergency – if only we had known! Only one worked, and I stationed it by the Mount, now the Tower, in the middle of the garden to supplement the others. We forgot about it until, as the audience was reassembling for the second half of the concert, with the rain once more beginning to pour down, Joy's nephew Julian Darker asked me if I knew that there was a floodlight still working. It was of course the Watsons' which Julian retrieved and installed in the stable to provide a beautiful spotlight for the piano.

Bernard then completed his programme and the guests, or most of them we think, went home contented.

It is a tribute to our soil drainage that next day, a beautiful Sunday open day, one would not have known there had been a drop of rain.

As a sequel to this, one of our more ambitious stable events was notable among other things for the high wind which brought down an electric cable, this

The stable. *Berberis valdiviana* on the left

time long enough beforehand for us to be prepared, so it was candles again. It was an Elizabethan evening of verse and music followed by a venison feast for which a whole deer was roasted in the yard (incidentally the heat and the dripping fat on the cobbles have proved to be the best weedkiller we have ever found). Most people in the audience thought that the candle lighting had been prearranged. In fact our friend Michael James (one of those two builders of last year) had spent all day installing elaborate electric lighting, so his feelings can perhaps be imagined when he heard one lady saying to another after the performance, 'and the lighting could not have been better'. It was Nyria James (Joy's bridesmaid) who arranged this entertainment. The feast in our candlelit tea room was much enjoyed, and one woman commented in a letter of thanks on various things including the buckets of syllabub and the three old sisters sitting opposite her – they were our friends Miss Harriett and the late Miss Joan Neill, and Mrs Nancy Radford who had dressed for the occasion as only they could.

The word climacteric presages some falling away which is one reason I used it. It wasn't that we felt that we had quite reached it in the medical sense, but for various other reasons we decided that any future functions of that kind should take place in the tea room. We like to think of our stable concerts which all take place in the summer and early autumn as something between public events and more intimate private soirées, and having come to know a lot of young musicians we started thinking of having musical parties of the latter type in the house, which was our main reason for extending the drawing room. We manage to seat about 25–30 comfortably and informally round the room with the artists near the middle of the longest wall. Starting with the inevitable Bernard King and Myra Chahin we have been delighted by the Platt Singers with Geoffrey Uffindel, Fiona and William Cuthbertson, Tom Kanter, Sheelagh Burns, Peter Croser, Dirik Jackson and Jeremy Carter, and usually after the arranged items others too numerous to mention.

I must record four things about Hogmanay 1978. Two-thirds of our guests couldn't get here because of the snow. We were enthralled by the playing of Edward Moulton-Barrett's friend, Arthur Ozolins, the celebrated pianist from Toronto, and what a privilege to hear such playing in our drawing room. For the third time in our history all the lights went out, this time about half past eleven, and to round off this chapter in a lighter vein, there is the tale of our first footers. After a lot of scuffling noises outside the door there arrived a gigantic model of a foot 7ft long, brought all the way from Sevenoaks in the deep snow on top of a car by 'Prof' Peter Fox and Sean Goodman, and introduced by Peter as only the first foot.

Great Comp in the XVIIth century

The map on page 121 dated about 1750 gives some indication of the size of the house and the farm buildings then and possibly for more than 100 years previously, as the house had been occupied by tenants for most of that time, and it is rather unlikely that they would have been allowed to make major alterations. We do not know definitely who built the house or when, although it is almost certain that the present house was built by Sir John Howell in the early part of the XVIIth century. John Newman suggests c1600, perhaps a fragment of a larger house. He mentions the mullioned and transomed windows, linked together by hood moulds continuing as string courses, an un-Kentish idiosyncrasy. It certainly appears to us that the existing XVIIth century part would hardly have been adequate for a knight owning more than 600 acres in Kent and land in Sussex. An architect visitor dated it c1625 as many of the bricks are of the larger size decreed by Charles I in that year, and unlikely to have been used before that. It is fairly certain that the present owners are not the first to have used old materials as I have measured bricks of all sizes between $1\frac{3}{4}$in and $2\frac{3}{4}$in in many parts of the house, outbuildings and garden walls, and all we can be sure of is that Great Comp as it stands today is a fine old hotch potch concocted over a period of more than 350 years.

For the name we need to go back to the XIIIth century and before. Comp was known as Camp de Wrothā (an abbreviation for Wrotham) in 1240, Caumpes in 1251 and Compe in 1461, and the name is derived from Old English Camp meaning campus or field (Glover/Wallenberg). An interesting footnote in the Rev. C. H. Fielding's book about Malling appears to suggest another possible but rather far-fetched derivation of the name. 'All kinds of food except bread and drink were called companage. In the time of Mary Wade, widow, there was given one parcel of ground to fynde a compe in the church of Trottiscliffe, also two garden plotts to fynde two compes one in the church and the other in the chancell.' William Lambarde states that Westcombe in Greenwich is so called because of the Danish army camp at nearby Blackheath c1012, 'for Comb and Compe in Saxon (being somewhat declined from Campus in Latine) signifieth a field or campe for an armie to sojourne in.' Hasted also suggests a military connection:

> About half a mile southward from Wrotham Heath, in the road from thence to Mereworth walks, is a district in which there are TWO SMALL HAMLETS situated on the summit of the hill, called GREAT and LITTLE COMP, and more vulgarly CAMPS, no doubt from their having been once made use of as camps, and probably by the Romans, their military way running towards their camp at OLDBERRY, and to STONE-street, at a small distance only from these places. Their name denotes their origin, Comp in Saxon signifying a camp or fortification.
>
> The country hereabouts is wild and rough ground, covered with bushes and small scrubby trees, and near adjoining southward to them is the great tract of woodland called Comp and the Herst woods. There was probably a chapel belonging to this district, the remains of which are still visible, being a chapel of ease to Leybourne, and built on a part of the glebe belonging to that rectory, on which account this land though separated by two parishes intervening, is now esteemed as being within the bounds of Leyborne parish.

114

SPRING
AND
AUTUMN

Left: View of the ruins.
Heathers in March with the yellow
Euphorbia myrsinites on the mound

Autumn with three of our tall limes,
Tilia x europaea

Spring in the ground acquired in 1962. Note *Magnolia salicifolia* on the left

Magnolia stellata, Rhododendron 'Yellowhammer' and Rhododendron 'Elizabeth'. The rhododendrons 'Blue Diamond' and 'Blue Tit' were transplanted only a week or so before the picture was taken. Legitimate instant gardening as they have not looked back since

Right. Almost the same view as on page 12, in autumn

There is more in Hasted's chapter on Leyborne. 'At a place called Comp lying mostly in Wrotham parish there is a small house and barnyard with about 130 acres of land, parcel of Leyborne Rectory, esteemed to be within this Parish, those of Ryarsh and Addington intervening. In part of it there are ruins of an ancient building supposed to have been a Chapel of Ease to the Church of Leyborne.' There is no trace of the chapel today, and it has certainly nothing to do with our ruins! The small house and barnyard are probably part of the golf course buildings.

How part of Great Comp came to be in Leybourne parish is an interesting story which like many good stories starts with a murder. Sir Roger de Leybourne was 'our great Kentish baron' much involved in the Barons' Wars in the reign of Henry III, sometimes siding with Simon de Montfort and sometimes with the King. In 1252 at Walden, Essex, he slew Arnold de Montigny against whom he was tilting. Although he said he was sorry he was suspected of murderous intent, as his lance point was uncovered, and it was remembered he had had his leg broken by Arnold in a joust. He was pardoned by the King, and Fielding suggests that his generous benefactions to Leybourne Church may have been an atonement for the murder. He gave lands from his estate in Leybourne and Caumpes to the Church. As recently as 1893 Fielding says, 'The lands at Caumpes, 100 acres, still belongs to the glebe of Leybourne.' In a footnote he adds that Great Comp Wood and Comp are still where there is a detached portion of Leybourne. There is no mention of Leybourne glebe in any of the Comp deeds we have seen of 1606 onwards, but in 1622 part of the estate adjoined land of the Bishop of Rochester. It is certain that part of the estate including part of the present garden was in Leybourne parish until it was transferred to Offham parish in this century (see map page 83).

Sir Roger was Warden of the Cinque Ports, and second on the list of those English knights who agreed to contribute loans towards the expenses of Prince Edward (later Edward I) on an expedition to the Holy Land. His contribution was 1,000 marks. He died in Palestine in 1271, and his heart is enshrined in Leybourne Church. On 25th October 1286, Edward I and his Queen (Queen Eleanor of my wife's Geddington Cross) visited Sir William, the son of his old friend and comrade in arms, and two iron crowns in the church are said to be votive gifts on that occasion. Sir William, who died in 1309, was, in 1297, appointed Admiral of the Sea of the King of England, the first use of the title in England. A modern wooden tablet in the church records that 'he gave land at Comp for mass to be said in this church for his parents Sir Roger and Lady de Leybourne'. An article from the *Church Times* framed in the church suggests that Sir Roger, dying in Palestine of wounds or sickness, might have made this last request which his son faithfully carried out.

Sir Roger's great granddaughter, Juliana, was the Kentish Bess of Hardwick of the XIV century. She outlived two husbands and also inherited from her grandfather, her father, Sir Thomas (died 1307), and her uncle, Sir Henry (died 1329), a most disreputable character and an outlaw. She died at Preston-next-Wingham on 1st November 1367 without issue leaving £3,160 13s 4d, an enormous sum for those days, and was known as the Infanta of Kent from the greatness of her possessions, most of which escheated to Edward III, including Yotes Court near Mereworth.

Above: A young Liquidambar in September

119

Below: Autumn colour by the front terraces.
Note the cotoneaster and *Sorbus hupehensis* berries

We do not know if the actual site of the present house was ever owned by the de Leybourne family or the King, and we have to wait another two hundred years for the next clue. It is stated on a table in Wrotham Church that:

Edward Dodge formerly of Lachlade in the County of Gloucester deceased did by his laft Will and Testament bearing date the 18th December 1597 (amongst other things) give as follows—'Item I give to the poor at Wrotham Five Pounds by the Year to be taken out of my Lands there. NB, This rent-charge is ifsuable out of a certain farm and Lands called Great Comp in the faid Parifh of Wrotham belonging to Multon Lambarde Efq^r. and now in the Occupation of Mr. Charles Style.'

WILLIAM LUCK—Churchwarden   July 1801

In the Wrotham church records the burial is recorded on 15th June 1579 of Thomas Greene, servant to Mr Dodge, but there is also a John Dodge mentioned in the Ightham Court records of 1546 and 1553–74. Where Edward lived and whether he or his men were involved at Blacksole Field Wrotham when Sir Robert Southwell and Lord Abergavenny and five hundred gentlemen and yeomen routed rebels under Sir Henry Isley of Sundridge in Wyatt's rebellion in the reign of Mary Tudor we do not know, but it is very likely that Great Comp was acquired after his death by a gentleman called John Howell, whom we have known about for over twenty years, but only from Hasted as having descended out of Sussex, and from entries in the Wrotham church register the burials on 12th May 1635 of Jane Lady and wife of Sir John Howell Knight and on 7th August 1641 of Sir John Howell Knight. Now we have found out so much more about him that I feel as if I almost knew him personally. The first reference in the deeds we have seen is in an indenture of 1664 which includes land conveyed to him on 13th March 1600, that is a little more than two years after Edward Dodge's will. (I have used the various spellings in the indentures.)

John Howell (later Sir John Howell) was the great grandson of John Howell of Sussex who married the daughter and heir of Thomas Seeles alias Gynnour also of Sussex in the reign of Henry VI. His two sisters married two brothers from Wrotham called Lucke which suggests that his parents lived in Wrotham. The earliest Howell record in the church register is the marriage of William Allen to Helen ap Howell on 6th August 1571 and could refer to an aunt.

Soon after he came to Great Comp he began to acquire more land. The same indenture of 1664 contains details of 16 items totalling about 430 acres and then refers to land conveyed at various dates from 1600 onwards from eight different people. We have seen and copied five of these eight indentures which include more than 199 acres making, with the other three we have not seen, appreciably more than 630 acres of the Comp estate at its probable maximum extent.

The earliest, Sir Thomas Vavasour Knight and Mary his wife, to John Howell dated 13th March 1600, we have not seen.

The first of the five we have seen dated 24th September 1606 is for a house and 13 acres at Little Comp called in the deed Compe Chappell (cf. Sir Roger de Leybourne). It was occupied by John Wickenden and the boundaries referred to include the main part bounded by the Highway leading from Plott to Offham, to the north, the Highway leading from Nepecker to Mereworth to the east and land of John Howell to the south and west, and four parcels bounded

120

LABORNE GLEBE

COMMON

North

South

Mr. Smith's land

Long Thirgoos
13 . 0 . 9
foot way

Little Thirgoos
9 . 1 . 32

Neamans
12 . 3 . 9

Wallnut-tree fd.
3 . 3 . 10

Bears Court

Bartholmew
9 . 0 . 29

Elleven acres
11 . 1 . 17

Parish Boundary

Smith

Furz field
13 . 2 . 6

Conduit-bank
14 . 1 . 14

Brickkiln fd.
6 . 1 . 9

Hemp place
0 . 2 . 0

18

4

Orchard
4 . 1 . 20

Usse field
9 . 3 . 53

Lit: Black-smith
8 . 2 . 30

Great Blacksmith
9 . 3 . 9

High Haught
14 . 1 . 20

Jams Croft
A 3 38

Brislo field
A . 1 . 30

Laborne Bartholmew 39

COMMON

A 0 . 10

Potters-hole
78 . 3 . 38

Sai: Baker, next Beauths

5 . 3 . 20

0 . 9

0 . 12

0 . 12

Broom field
26

Pgeons greens

Mr. Strange
Furze field
Furze Hillway

Viccaridge
3 . 2 . 4

North

A MAP of part of Great Comp and a farm at
Pigeons-Green: and Two Cottages, lying in the Parishes of
Wrotham and Laborne in the County of KENT

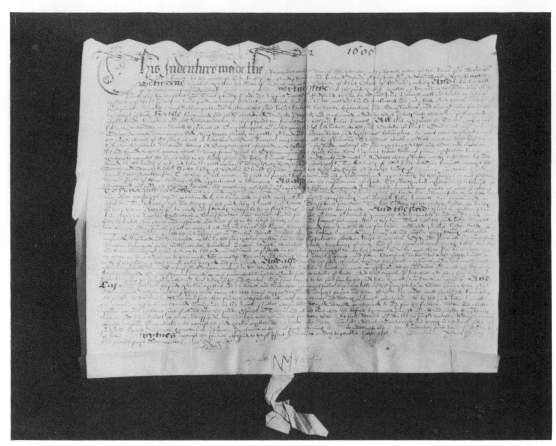

Indenture of 1606. Nicholas Myller to John Howell

by land of John Howell and land belonging to Sir John Leveson, William Clerke Esquier and Thomas Watton Esquier. The consideration was the sum of fouer score and tenne pounde of good and lawfull money of England. The vendor was Nicholas Miller (spelt Myller) the elder who lived at Crouch then called Horsenayles Crouch who died in 1622 and whose burial place is marked by a floor slab in Wrotham church. Horsenayles or Horsnells is a mediaeval word for tadpoles and the name was dropped in the XVIIth century. In place of a signature there is at the bottom of the indenture 'NM the mke of Nicolas Myller'. From Hasted this Nicholas is probably the Nicholas Miller gent. to whom Sir Thomas Colepeper, of Preston Hall, alienated the manor of Sore (now Old Soar) about the end of the reign of Queen Elizabeth. In the Wrotham register the burials are recorded of two of his probable ancestors, William Miller the elder on 22nd October 1589 (father?) and John Miller of Horsenaile Crotch ye elder on 23rd April 1570 (grandfather?). Sore passed to his son Nicholas Miller, Esq. of Horsnells Crouch who in the beginning of James I's reign acquired Wingfield manor from James Peckham, Esq. of Yaldham, three small manors, Dencrouch, Highlands and Priggles, in Pembury from Sir Anthony Colepeper of Bedgbury, and (date not known) the manor of Oxenhoath from Sir George Chowne, of Fairlawne. This son of a father who could not sign his name was sheriff of Kent in 1633 and was apparently the principal founder of the extensive Miller estate which included all of Hurst woods and lands stretching down to Platt, Wrotham Heath and Basted. He died in 1640 and his son became Sir Nicholas Miller who died in 1658 and whose second son, the fourth Nicholas, resided at Horsnells Crouch which had been left to him by his grandfather the sheriff.

122

The second, which is in Latin, is dated 15th February 1607, John Wybarne conveying to John Howell, Claypits, Reedes and Ham in the Burgu of Nepacre (the modern Nepicar from the Saxon Naep – a turnip, aecer – a piece of cultivated ground).

In the third dated 10th April 1608 Francis Clarke of Dover conveyed to John Howell a house and land of seven acres in the parish of Leybourne occupied by John Wickenden and William Fyppes and bounded by the Kinges highe way leading from Town Maleing to Comp towards the south to the land of Edmund Clarke gent towards the north and east and to the highe way leading from Wrotham to Mereworth on the weste.

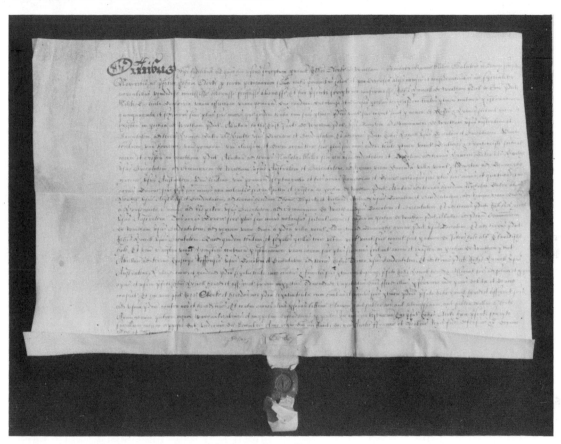

Deed of 1622. Sir John Clerke to Sir John Howell

The fourth and by far the most important is in Latin dated 11th September 1622 in which Sir John Clerke conveyed to Sir John Howell several houses and land totalling 157 acres. Sir John had therefore been knighted since the last deed of 1608.

The boundaries include land of the heirs of Nicholas Baker als Heath, the highway leading from Horsnells Crouch to Nepiker, common land of Wrotham, the King's highway leading from Addington to Borough Green, and land of the Bishop of Rochester. There is no sum mentioned and this transaction could well be connected with the marriage of Sir John Howell to Sir John Clerke's sister Jane. In the Herald's visitation of 1619 Jane Clerke is referred to as 'Jana desponsata Johis Howell de Compe in Wrotham Militi'. (ie Betrothed.)

In the last of the five dated 13th October 1631 Thomas Sperke, fuller, of Leybourne, in consideration of forty and three pounds of lawfull money of

123

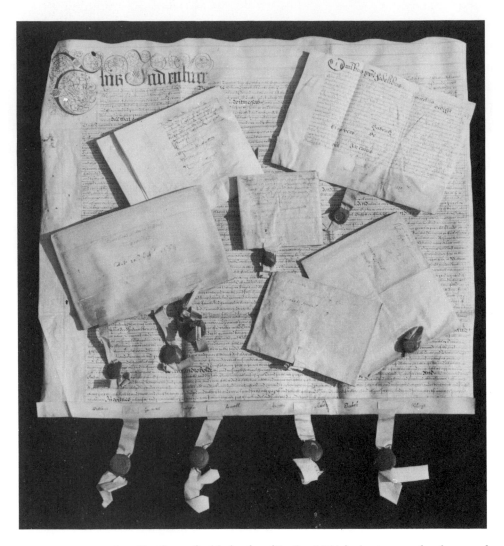

A collection of old deeds with the 1664 indenture as background

England conveyed to Sir John Howell some buildings and 13 acres of land; Samons (10 acres) neere to a certain sole or common watering place commonly called Courte Sole or Stand Sole abounding the Kinges Highway leading from Compe to Boroughe Greene towards the south and west and Suit (3 acres) also bounding to the aforesaid Kinges Highway towards the northe.

The other two we have not seen relate to land conveyed to Sir John Howell by Thomas Wybarne on 19th November 1631 and by George Segars gent. on 29th October 1636.

In the Wrotham church register is recorded on 2nd September 1571 the baptism of Jane daughter of Mr William Clerke who is most probably the William Clerke Esq. who died aged 75 on 23rd March 1612 and who with his wife Ann and two sons and ten daughters is commemorated in a small brass set in the floor of the church. The Clerkes had been established for many years at Ford Place part of which can still be seen from the M20 motorway. It is a nice thought that William, Ann and half a dozen young children might have greeted Queen Elizabeth after she had passed through Ightham on her way from Knole to Birling Manor in 1573. In the Ightham court records dated 8th February 1506 William's great grandparents John and Lucy complain of Hamo Wymbull for debt of 20p and in the following February an order was given to the bailiff to levy the goods and chattels to Hamo Wymbull for 19d, the principal debt and

124

The Clerke Brass in St George's Church, Wrotham. One of the 10 daughters, Jane, married Sir John Howell

6d for expenses and costs to the court, to the use of John Clerke, gent. The Clerkes had been at Ford for at least two generations before that.

And so about the year 1620 Sir John Howell having inherited land in Sussex acquired his medium-sized estate in Kent, and built part of the present house, married the sister of John Clerke of Ford, a woman of about fifty years of age. In the Herald's Visitation of 1619 it is John Clerke and John Howell so it looks as if both were knighted between 1619 and the deed of 1622. If Sir John Howell had any expectation of raising a family and an heir of his body he was quite soon to be disillusioned, and again the Wrotham registers supply the information. On 30th May 1627 was baptised John the son of Edward Howell als Lucke, and as Edward was Sir John's nephew the son of his sister Constance, and John Lucke, it appears that Sir John, having given up hope of having children of his own, had decided to make his nephew his heir. The change of name was quite a common occurrence at that time. Lady Jane died in 1635 and is buried at Wrotham and then for reasons we can only guess Sir John, having made his nephew his heir, decided to marry a younger woman in the hope of having a son of his own. His second wife was Sarah Brodnax, the second daughter of Thomas Brodnax of Godmersham, and they were married on 9th February 1641.

The manor of Ford in Godmersham was the property of the family Austen or

125

Astyn until conveyed to Thomas Brodnax (or Broadnax) from Hyth. In 1619, his son Thomas and nine of the latter's ten children were alive including Thomas, the eldest, a student in the Temple and Sarah, the seventh, who would therefore probably be no more than thirty in 1641. The story of the family of Thomas the law student is of considerable interest. A later Thomas, possibly his great grandson and Sarah's great great nephew, in 1727 pursuant to the will of Sir Thomas May and under the authority of Parliament changed his name to May. He rebuilt the Elizabethan manor house in 1732 and in 1738 pursuant to the will of Mrs Elizabeth Knight and under the authority of another Act changed his name again to Knight and in 1742 enclosed a park round his seat afterwards called Ford Park and later Godmersham Park. Thomas May Knight died advanced in years in 1781. His only married child, Thomas, greatly improved the house and park, died without issue in 1794 and left the estate to his wife for her lifetime and then to Edward Austen Esq. of Rolling Place who resided there after Mrs Knight had moved to White Friars in Canterbury. All this is from Hasted who, in 1798, would have no idea of the future implications of this story. Edward Austen who changed his name to Edward Austen Knight was Jane Austen's brother. Jane was a regular visitor to the house, she loved the park and is reputed to have written some of her novels there.

The Brodnaxes were obviously friends of William James of Ightham, as he was one of the trustees of Sarah's joynture. This interesting document '. . . witnesseth that the said Sir John Howell for and in consideration of five hundred pounds of lawfull English money to him well and truly paid by the said Thomas Brodnax the elder at and before the sealing and delivery of these presents for the marriage portion of her the said Sarah his said daughter . . .' In return Sir John covenanted to '. . . stand be seized of and in all that capital messuage with the appurtenances wherein the said Sir John Howell now dwelleth . . .'. The estate then consisted of '. . . the edifices buildings pidgeon house barns stables courts yards gardens orchards and closes thereunto belonging containing in the whole by estimation twelve acres more or lesse and of and in one close conteyning by estimation ten acres lying before the gate of the said messuage and of and in all those severall parcells of land arrable medowe pasture wood and heath grounds conteyning in the wholle by estimation two hundred fifty and five acres more or less lying and being in Wrotham aforesaid and now in the occupation of him the said Sir John Howell or of his assignes . . .'. Sir John was therefore farming less than half of his estate and the rest, also included in the joynture, was let to the following tenants: Isacke Parke, Richard Cladden, Robert Walter, John Isall, John Wickenden, widdowe Welch, John Phipps, Daniell Stephenson, Abram Psalter and Thomas Larkin. All other lands, etc, of Sir John in Wrotham were included 'fower acres of woodland be it more or less called Taylors Brookes in Wrotham aforesaid only excepted'. The Brodnaxes covenanted with Sir John '. . . if the said Sarah fortune to overlive the said Sir John Howell and after being a widdowe shall be resolved and determined to marry againe that then she the said Sarah before her said marriage shall make a good and sufficient lease . . .' (to Sir John's heirs of the estate) . . . 'for two hundred pounds per annum'.

Alas Sir John did not enjoy his new marriage for long, as he died in August the same year, soon after making his last will and testament. This is such an

126

Hasted *circa* 1798

127

interesting document including provision for the poor and his servants, evidence of family squabbles, the rather touching afterthought that he might still have a son, and a beneficiary witnessing his signature, that it is given in full as an appendix to this book. He refers to himself as aged which together with the fact that his first wife was born in 1571 suggests that he was probably over seventy when he died. His will was dated 11th June 1641, one month and one day after the King consented to the Bill by which Parliament could not be dissolved without its own consent, an event which, with others of the time, led his neighbour Sir Roger Twisden, of Roydon Hall, who had been one of the two Knights of the Shire in the previous Short Parliament, to wonder if the Long Parliament might become more tyrannical than the regime it set out to reform. Incidentally Sir Roger died of apoplexy whilst riding through the Mereworth Woods in 1672.

Although Sir John and his brother-in-law Sir John Clerke, who died in 1644, were no doubt important mid-Kent gentry (between them they probably owned most of the land between the Hurst Woods and Wrotham), I have found nothing in any of the books I have consulted to show how they or the Luckes or Great Comp itself fared in the troubled times of 1640–60 including the Great Civil War of 1642–48.

Sir John Sedley of St Clere with whom Sir John Howell had sat as a justice in 1633 was a prominent member of the Parliamentary Committee for Kent in 1643 and with the Brodnax's friend William James of Ightham Court Lodge was much involved in quelling the Royalist Rising at Sevenoaks in July 1643. On the other hand it was the refusal at the end of June of Sir John Howell's friend and beneficiary John Grimes the Ightham parson to take the oath of allegiance to Parliament which led directly to the Rising, and Lady Jane's nephew Sir William Clerke was one of the more extreme cavaliers who 'manifested his loyalty to the King by raising and arming a regiment at his own charge, at the head of which he was slain, together with Sir William Boteler, in the fight between the King's forces, and those of the parliament, under Sir William Waller, at Cropredy-bridge, on 29th June, 1644'. Again in the second rising in 1648 it is known that seven members of the Tomlyn family, neighbours at Nepicar, assembled with the royalist petitioners at Coxheath near Maidstone. All that I have read suggests that most of the landed gentry were moderates, that is basically royalists who, while admitting the errors of the King, soon recognised at least as great danger from an all powerful parliament, and it is quite likely that Sir John belonged to this category, just as his income appears to have been about the average of Kentish gentry, which according to Everett was about £650 per annum. In his will he left various sums adding up to not far short of £1,000, two annuities of £100 per annum each, and the Comp estate was worth another £200 per annum. As there was more land in Sussex and leases it is quite possible that his income exceeded £600 per annum which Abell estimates would have been worth about £3,000 per annum at the beginning of the present century. That is to say he was well enough off but nothing like as wealthy as, for example, Sir John Baker of Sissinghurst who was said in 1644 to have £2,500 a year.

But it was not Sir John, but his widow and the Luckes who had to contend with the troubles, and by 28th September 1641, only twenty-four days after Sir

128

John's will had been proved in London, Dame Sarah had left Great Comp and was 'at or in the nowe mansion house of William James Esquier commonlie called Ightham Court Lodge'. On that date she signed an indenture leasing the Comp estate to Edward Howell als Lucke for twenty-one years for a yearly rent of two hundred poundes to be paid quarterly at the four usual feasts or terms, that is the rent agreed in her joynture if she remarried. Whether she did so and when she died is not known, but Edward Howell als Lucke also left Great Comp and was living in London where he died in 1653, but was buried at Wrotham. His eldest son John died aged 31 in 1658 and, Robert and Edward and Dame Sarah also having died by 1664, the estate would have been inherited by the fourth son William born in 1633. As he was also the last surviving son of Edward and Frances and presumably had no children he was able to dispose of the Comp estate, but on 20th October 1664 he was not the sole owner as the indenture of sale of that date was between him, his wife Deborah, his sister Elizabeth and her husband Ambrose Milmay of Maidstone of the one part and Sir John Beale Bt. of Maidstone of the other part. Elizabeth was of course the sister to whom Sir John Howell had left £500 in 1641.

We have seen two copies of the indenture in one of which William is described as of the parish of St Martin in the Fields in the County of Middlesex *gent.*, and in the other, *baker*. Sir John Beale paid £1,500 for Great Comp and more than 630 acres. When Edward Howell als Lucke left he had let the house, 'commonly called or known by the name of Great Compe or Comp House', and farm of 250 acres to Valentine Nicholls als Holmesbie, and 30 acres of woodland. The farm 'commonly called or known by the name of Little Compe, or by whatsoever other name or names the same house is or hath been called or known' included in the sale extended to 69 acres and was let in parts to Valentine Nicholls als Holmesby, John Welsh and William Welsh, and had previously been let to Thomas Phipps, John Phipps and Edward Welsh, father of William. There was also 41 acres 'at or near to a certain place called Nepeker Burrough or Nepeker Streete', including a meadow called Vidians Mead, 28 acres at Wrotham Hoath, Holmebush House and 2 acres occupied by Daniel Tooth, and 7 more acres, all the above 'being in the several parishes of Wrotham, Ightham, Stanstead and Layborne'. There were also three adjacent houses near Wrotham Church occupied by James Sharpe, blacksmith, Thomas Cavill, and William Skynner, and $2\frac{3}{4}$ acres of land adjoining Cavill's house occupied by him and George Weston. Lastly there was all the land conveyed in the eight indentures previously mentioned, and altogether Sir John Beale got 630 acres plus the land included in the three indentures we have not seen and a number of houses including Great Comp itself, and his purchase ended for ever Sir John Howell's hopes of establishing an estate and line. There is another Sir John Howell buried at Ightham, Recorder of London, who died in 1682, but he is not connected with our Sir John.

Sir John Beale Bt., of an old Maidstone family, was born about 1621, created a baronet in 1660, High Sheriff of the County in 1665, and lived at East Court Manor, Farningham, when he died on 3rd October 1684. His first wife Anne, daughter of Sir William Culpepper Bt. of Aylesford, died in 1657, and it was his second wife Jane, daughter of Richard Duke, of Maidstone, who bore him four daughters who became his co-heirs. In a wall tablet in Farningham Church there is the following inscription: 'Near this place lies the body of William Hanger Esq. son of Sr. George Hanger of Dryfield in the county of Glocester Kt. by Dame Ann his wife daughter and co-heiress of Sir John Beal Bar' of this place. He died the 30th of January 1751 aged 48. By J. Pickford.' Sir John was a considerable landowner and left his Farningham estate to his daughter Elizabeth who married William Emerton Esq. of Chipstead. His daughter Jane married Sir Thomas Roberts, Bt., of Glassenbury. In addition to the parts his other daughters would have inherited, '. . . the said Sir John Beale in and by his last will and testament bearing date the thirtieth day of Aprill in the year 1683 among other devises therein mentioned to his daughters did devise to the said Mary in the following manner – I give unto my daughter Mary Beale all that my lands and tenements in the Isle of Sheppey and my lands and tenements in Wrotham I bought of Mr. Howell'. The quotation is from an indenture which brings a new and highly important name into the Great Comp history. In December 1694 a marriage settlement was arranged between William Lambarde of Sevenoaks in the county of Kent Esq. and Magdalen his wife, and Thomas Lambarde eldest son of the said William Lambarde of the one part and Sir Thomas Roberts Bart., William Emerton Esq. and Mary the wife of the said Thomas Lambarde by the name of Mary Beale one of the daughters of Sir John Beale Bart., deceased of the other part, in which Mary, although under age agreed that inter alia the Comp estate should be limited to her for her life for her joynture, and thereafter to Thomas Lambarde and his heirs. The business was complicated, however, in legal ways beyond the comprehension of the present writer, but needing an 'Act of Parliament made and passed in the fifth yeare of the reigne of her late Majestie Queen Ann intitueled an act for the more effectual assureing of pte of the lande of inheritance of Wm and Thomas Lambard in the County of Kent persuant to a deed of settlement and for assureing (in liew of other parte thereof) other lands of inheritance therein also mentioned and for better provision for younger children', to remove 'certeyne doubts' that might arise. So Mary Beale, at the age of 20, married Thomas Lambarde in 1695, and all this information is contained in a tripartite indenture of sale dated 26th October 1715 of part of the estate by Thomas Lambarde and Mary his wife of the first part and Percivall Hart of Lullingstone Esq. only surviving trustee named in and by the Act of Parliament hereinafter mentioned of the second part to Isaac Tomlyn of Wrotham in the said county of Kent yeoman of the third part. (The other trustees were Sir Tho Roberts, Wm Emmerton and Sir Thomas Twisden of East Peckham Barront). Isaac Tomlyn paid seven hundred thirty three pounds and three shillings of lawfull money of Greate Brittaine to Thomas Lambarde and five shillings to Percivall Hart for 46 acres previously occupied by John Harper and now by Thomas Cotton, three other little fields containing about 4 acres and a half late in the possession of the widdow Broad since John Harper but now Thomas Cotton and a field called Hamsfield containing 6 acres previously occupied by Robert Hunt and now by Thomas Cotton. So the nearly two hundred years of Lambarde ownership of Great Comp started with a small dismantling of the estate and incidentally of a marked increase in the Tomlyn activities. The present handsome sashed house at Nepicar occupied by Mr Tomlyn in 1798 is dated by Newman c1700, so Isaac was doing well.

130

The Lambardes 1694–1874

William Lambarde, the author of the earliest county history of England, *The Perambulation of Kent,* written in 1570, was the son of John Lambarde, draper, alderman and sheriff of London in 1551. William was also an important lawyer and author of several legal books. His father bought the Manor of Westcombe in Greenwich during the reign of Mary I. The Manor House was near the junction of the present Vanbrugh Hill and Westcombe Park Road, and was demolished about 1725. In 1570 while William was publishing his draft of the *Perambulation* he was also courting his future bride, the 16-year-old daughter of George Multon, owner of the Manor of St Clere. The moiety of St Clere had belonged to Sir Thomas Bulleyn, the father of Anne, wife of Henry VIII, who sold it to Richard Farmer who owned the whole estate and in 1536 conveyed it to George Multon (Hasted), but according to Retha M. Warnicke St Clere was granted by the Crown to Mr Multon, then of Hadlow, in 1547. The present St Clere, formerly called St Clere's, was built about 1633 by Sir John Sedley, the notable Parliamentarian and Sir John Howell's fellow Justice. He had acquired the Manor from George Multon's grandson. In modern times St Clere was the residence of Lord Norman, better known as Montagu Norman the famous Governor of the Bank of England. William Lambarde chose to live with his wife's family after his wedding on 11th September 1570 to Jane Multon on the eve of her 17th birthday. She died childless after six days' illness, probably smallpox, on 21st September 1573, and for the next ten years William continued to live at St Clere. There is a fragment of a memorial to Jane in Ightham Church. His second marriage was in 1583 to Sylvestria Dalyson of Halling, widow of Sir William Dalyson, by whom he had four children, all of interest. The eldest was Multon, a lawyer, who wrote on 11th February 1608, 'It pleased His Majestie to bestowe ye honoure of knighthood upon mee at Whitehall as he passed through the gallery to ye chapell,' the first of many Multon Lambardes, but one of the only two Lambardes to be given a title. Margaret, his daughter, married Thomas Godfrey and their son Lambarde Godfrey was a notable Roundhead in and around Maidstone during and after the Civil War. Twins Gore and Fane, born in 1587 the year Sylvestria died, apparently both died fairly young and will be mentioned again later. The Dalysons lived in the Bishop's Palace, Halling, a substantial part of a wall of which can still be seen close to the church. In the church is a brass commemorating Silvester (Sylvestria) on which she is shown sitting up in a four poster bed. There are twins in a cradle beside her and the inscription says *'Gemelliparae positum'.* During the whole of this marriage William resided at Halling, the home of his second wife and her father Robert Dene, and then returned to Greenwich. He married a third time (Margaret Reader without issue) and died in 1601. He played a prominent part in Kentish affairs, for example he and Sir John Leveson, Sir John Howell's neighbour, were two of the trustees of Rochester Bridge, and he was involved in a survey of Otford Manor and House, presumably part of the Palace which Henry VIII left in favour of Knole as it was too damp.

Sir Multon died in 1634 and his son and heir Thomas was a considerable man who according to different accounts was a great Royalist (Hasted) and later an out and out Puritan (Ward), but I think this is unlikely, and I have found no other reference of him being anything but a Royalist. He agreed to compound for his estate and as a result had to sell Westcombe and move to Squerryes Court, Westerham, on 9th November 1649. But he was still a man of wealth as he paid £8,500 for Squerryes Court and 424 acres called Panthers Parke, Sevenoaks. Then in 1654 he sold Squerryes Court and purchased Sevenoaks Park and the Manor of Rumshed for £2,580, starting the Lambardes' association with Sevenoaks which lasted for more than 300 years. Curiously enough the first page of the Sevenoaks church register contains an entry dated 7th February 1559 of the baptism of Dorytie Lambarde. Thomas resided in Sevenoaks Park and diverted the road to keep the traffic away from his house, hence the sudden big bend in the Tonbridge Road opposite Knole Park. Sevenoaks Park is the present Park Grange.

Thomas died in 1675 and his son William and his wife Magdalen became the first Lambardes to have an interest in Great Comp through the marriage settlement of their son and heir Thomas and Mary Beale. William and Magdalen had another son who became the second Lambarde knight at the Coronation of George II, and through his wife Jane Fowler the Lambardes became patrons of Ash church which they are to this day. Lady Jane lived near Sevenoaks Vine and died as late as 1780, her husband having been born in 1676.

On 7th January 1719 'Thomas Lambarde of Sevenoakes Esquire' signed a lease of Great Comp to 'Isaac Tomlyn of Nepikar yeoman' for a term of 21 years. The annual rent was £71 8s to be paid in two equal portions. The land consisted of 195 acres on the south part or side of Wrotham Heath in the parish of Wrotham and in the parish of Layborne lately occupied by Robert Hunt and now by Isaac Tomlyn himself, 60 acres usually let with Great Compe on the north west part of Wrotham Heath lately occupied by Robert Hunt and now by Isaac Tomlyn, and a cottage occupied by the widow Tapsfield.

The indenture is a lengthy document some of which is worth quoting. Thomas Lambarde retained the timber, the right to inspect at any time 'the condition of the decays and wants of reparations and amendments', to hunt and 'the game therehad and taken to have take and carry away at his and their wills and pleasures doing as little damage as maybe', the use for passage of the 'high heath conduit bank Great Thurgoes part of the said demised premises', two acres now fenced off occupied by John Berry, and 'four acres of land more lying on the North west corner of the said High Heath which it shall and may be lawful att any time during this demise for the said Thomas Lambard his heires or assignes to fence off and inclose when he or they shall think fitt'. Isaac Tomlyn was permitted 'to break up for tillage that part or parcell of land whereon the Barn stands in the lower land for and during the first eleven yeares of the terme of this demise . . .' but for every acre of 'New Mead or Five Acre Mead the Six Acre Mead and the Eleven Acre Mead which shall be ploughed sowed digged broken up or converted into tillage during the term hereby demised (other than what is hereby agreed to be broken up for the first eleven years of the said term) the yearly rent or summe of five pounds of lawfull money of Great Brittaine over and above the yearly rent herein-before reserved and so proportionably for every greater or lesser quantity than an acre thereof to be paid . . .'. The buildings were to be maintained of course and Mr Tomlyn had to '. . . well and sufficiently repaire uphold sustaine maintaine amend and keep well and sufficiently repaired all the said demised messuage or tenement and cottage barnes stables buildings and outhouses in and upon the said demised premisses in by and with all and all manner of needful and necessary reparations and amendments whatsover and likewise shall and will (when need shall require) at his and their like proper costs and charges well and sufficiently make amend repaire scower cleanse and keep all and every the posts pales railes gates barrs stiles hedges ditches fences and inclosures in about or belonging to the same messuage cottage lands and premisses or any part thereof he and they planting with quick sett all the dead places in the said fences . . .'.

The indenture continues: 'AND also that he the said Isaac Tomlyn his executors administrators and assignes shall and will inne and lay in the barnes and buildings hereby demised or otherwise sett in stacks or ricks on the said demised premisses all the corn graine hay clover and fodder which shall yearly grow be mowed reaped or had in or upon the said lands and premisses during the term aforesaid and the straw of all the said corn and all the said hay clover and fodder shall and will in good husbandlike manner yearly fodder spend and sewe out in and upon the said lands and premisses or some part thereof and not elsewhere within the said term otherwise and excepting tenn loads of hay or straw which it is hereby agreed the said Isaac Tomlyn his executors administrators and assignes may have liberty to sell and carry off yearly from the said premisses provided he and they for each and every load of hay or straw so carried off do bring and lay down and in good husbandlike manner spread upon the meadow lands hereby demised two loads of small chalk each load or carriage to consist of sixty bushells and also that he the said Isaac Tomlyn his executors administrators and assignes shall and will yearly and every year during the said term in good husbandlike manner lay bestow expend and spread upon the land and premisses hereby demised or some part thereof and not elsewhere all the dung muck soyle sullage and compost which shall arise be cast out or made in upon or about the said premisses from time to time during the term aforesaid'. There is much about timber and fruit trees and hops which had to be protected from 'all hurt brutt and destruction of cattell or otherwise'. Mr Lambarde provided any young fruit trees required. At the end of the term for every acre not planted with hops as required Mr Tomlyn had to pay the sum of ten pounds. If Isaac Tomlyn 'shall plough break up and sow with corn the said demised landes and premisses or any part thereof in the last seven years of the term of this demise three times that then he or they shall and will well and sufficiently ameild the same with lime well burnt or dung and for such ameildment thereof he or they shall and will provide bring lay spread and in good and husbandlike manner bestowe on each and every acre thereof so to be ploughed broken up or sowed the number and quantity of one load or carriage and a half of good chalke lime two loads or carriages of good stone lyme each carriage of lime to consist and containe sixty bushels or else sixty cartloads of good dung . . .'. At the end of the term there had to be left 30 acres of clover of one year's growth and if Thomas Lambarde thought fit 'in the last year of the said term hereby demised to make or cause to be made thirty acres of the said demised premisses for sum or fallow viz tenn acres of the land called the lower land ten acres of the lands adjoining to and about the said messuage and ten acres of the other land he and they paying and allowing to the said Isaac Tomlyn his executors administrators and assignes at the rate of tenn shillings per acre for the said low land eight shillings per acre for the land adjoining to and about the said messuage and five shillings per acre for the other land so made into fallow.'Isaac Tomlyn 'shall and will yearly and every year during the term of this demise bear pay and discharge one annuity or yearly rent charge of five pounds of lawfull money called or known by the name of Dodges Guift yearly issuing and payable out of the said demised premises to the said parish of Wrotham'. Altogether this deed contains quite a lot of interest concerning estate management in the early XVIIIth century.

Of course we do not know who actually lived in Great Comp house, perhaps one of Isaac's family, as he would be in his fine house at Nepicar. Isaac Tomlyn died in 1741.

Most of the XVIIth century Lambardes were buried at Greenwich and a memorial to William and his son Sir Multon was erected to them both in the church after the latter's death in 1634. When the church was demolished to make way for the St Alphage of Nicholas Hawksmoor the Lambarde monument was removed to Sevenoaks Church by Thomas Lambarde in 1733 and an inscription under it reads,

'Curante Thoma Lambard Arm^{ro}
Guilielmii Filo
Thomae Nepote
An. Dom. MDCCXXXIII.'

The other Thomas would be the elder brother of William who died before his father.

Thomas Lambarde died in 1745 and was succeeded by his son also Thomas. The two maps *circa* 1750 (pages 121 and 143) show part of his estate. There are two other maps and a sheet headed 'The Contents' which make up an attractive booklet in the Kent County Archives.

The Contents

	A	R	P
Bassetts Farm	34	2	15
Two cottages A and B	7	2	38
Great Comp	281	1	1
Two cottages C and D	1	1	12
Farm at Pigeon's Green	11	1	31
Little Comp	79	0	20
	415	1	37

This is presumably the extent of the Lambarde property at Comp, ie the Comp Estate in the mid XVIIIth century. There are some fields they owned by Pigeons Green, one curiously named Suett, which as we have seen was acquired by Sir John Howell in 1631. A century later they gave some of the fields for the erection of a church and to provide a glebe. This is not the Pigeons Green we know today, which is further up Comp Lane. There is no trace now of three of the four buildings to the west of our drive, but the bottom one may be the barn which we believe to be as old as our house, partly because of the similar roof structure. The fifth one shown to the west of it may be the old cart shed which

Acer 'Osakazuki', *Evodia hupehensis* and
Quercus rubra in autumn

Hosta undulata in the ruin

Mixed borders with Hypericum 'Hidcote', rose 'Albertine' and, further along, one of

also still exists. The top one is certainly not the present Gate Cottage which was presumably built in the Maxwells' time, and for a time owned and occupied by the Fishendens, as it is not shown on the plan of the whole estate of 1905. It is also interesting to note that there is no sign on the map of the house now called Old Comp. This was built before 1905 and used to be known as Park Cottage, and before that Seers Cottage. It has been much extended in recent years. It is also interesting to note that there is no sign of our outbuildings, and where The Oasts now stand there is only one rectangular building. The making of such a map could have been in connection with a new lease after the expiry of Isaac Tomlyn's in 1739 or his death in 1741 and it is certain that, with the boundary hedge nearly touching the house, the setting of Great Comp as shown was not the residence of a gentleman. It looks as if the house was approached through the farmyard, not at all unlikely if it was occupied by tenant farmers, even of a somewhat superior class. Although alterations would be taking place continuously, as indeed they still are, my present belief is that the main outbuildings, Seers Cottage, The Oasts and the drive with its avenue of limes all date from the 19th century. At that time also three of the fairly substantial buildings shown on the map (which are not shown on the 1819 Ordnance Survey map) would have been demolished and the materials used to construct the present buildings, and as hardcore for a new drive. The building we use in the summer as a tea room on open days and for coffee after concerts has been dated by a visitor as about the end of the 18th century because of the type of roof, but of course the construction could easily have been used 20 or 30 years later. The stable when it was first built had a hip-ended roof, later altered to the present gable. I believe round oast houses were not built before about 1820.

The family of Thomas Lambarde, who died in 1770, has a distinctly Jane Austen look about it. None of the four daughters was married in his or his wife's lifetime, and by 1783 one can imagine Multon, the head of the family, much exercised about his unmarried sisters and his brother Thomas. Anyway two years later all were married except the eldest, 39-year-old Grace, the other three sisters to parsons including one with the evocative name of Sackville Austen, and brother Thomas having become a parson himself, rector of Ash in 1782. Thomas married Sophia Otway and in 1789 Multon himself married Sophia's sister Aurea. Multon Lambarde resided at Sevenoaks Park which is charmingly described in the diary of Miss Jane Edwards (1792–1869) 'Multon Lambarde lived here when I was a little girl. It was a very pretty old-fashioned stone mansion with a pretty lawn and beautiful flowers and a stately peacock marching about at his pleasure. There was a low boxed-hedge round it and two little low white gates so that passers-by had a good view of the mansion. Mr and Mrs Lambarde were highly respected by all the neighbouring gentry. They were much noticed by the Duchess of Dorset. I have seen the two elder Miss Lambardes walking in the park with the Duchess and her two daughters once or twice (this was when they were young) . . . but since that time many changes have taken place and the pretty house was sold to Colonel Austen of Kippington who had the principal part taken down and the other part made into a farm house'. Jane Austen was 13 when the last of the marriages took place and would certainly have known the Lambardes and Sevenoaks Park. It is a nice fancy to think that later on in her journeying from Sevenoaks to Godmersham to visit her relations she might have actually visited a Lambarde at Great Comp, but I am afraid it is not very likely.

It is the marriage of Jane Lambarde, the youngest sister to the Revd. John Randolph, DD, which concerns Great Comp. John Randolph was the grandson of Herbert Randolph, Recorder of Canterbury. In 1776 he was professor of poetry at Oxford University, Regius Professor of Greek, professor of moral philosophy, and in 1783 Regius Professor of Divinity with a canonry of Christ Church Cathedral and rectory of Ewelme. His divinity lectures were delivered by candlelight, most of the undergraduates slept, and the only things carried away were the syllabus given to reach student at the beginning and a formidable list of authors for future reading which was supplied at the close. I have read that he used a whistle to keep them awake. He became Bishop of Oxford in 1789, of Bangor in 1807 and of London in 1809, and is buried in Fulham churchyard.

One day during this past winter we spent some time in Platt churchyard to see what we could find from the tombstones and in particular we were looking for the tomb of one we had known of for many years as Captain Randolph, the first churchwarden of Platt Church and the owner of Great Comp. We seemed to be searching in vain when my wife found just behind the east end of the church under a yew tree and obscured by brambles and grass a simple but dignified horizontal tombstone surrounded by a low iron railing with the following inscriptions on either side of the bevelled top:

CHARLES GRENVILLE RANDOLPH
ADMIRAL ROYAL NAVY DIED 1ST MAY 1871 AGED 77 YEARS

JULIA WIFE OF ADMIRAL RANDOLPH DIED 21ST JANY 1876 AGED 81 YEARS.

The man we had assumed to be an army captain (he had never been given the letters RN in any of our references) was in fact a naval officer who had served with distinction in the Napoleonic Wars and here surely was a case of '. . . now lies he there, and none so poor to do him reverence'. This we hope to rectify by at least keeping the grave tidy.

We now of course suspected that he was the son of the Bishop, and to find out more about him we could think of nowhere better than the National Maritime Museum in Greenwich. Having looked at all the paintings in this wonderful place in case he might by chance have appeared in one of them we then found what we wanted in the Library in the first line of his entry in *Modern English Biographies* by F. Boase. 'Randolph Charles Grenville (3 son of John Randolph 1749–1813 Bishop of London) b.1793 . . .'. He was educated at Westminster and entered the Royal Navy as a midshipman in 1806 on board the *Donegal 74* commanded by Captain (later Sir Pulteney) Malcolm under whom he served for nearly five years, principally in the Channel Station. In 1808 he witnessed one of the significant moments of European history, the landing of the British Army under Sir Arthur Wellesley on the shores of Portugal, and in February 1809 the destruction of three French frigates in the Sable d'Ollone, on which occasion the *Donegal* had seven men killed or wounded: he was also present at the memorable attack made upon the enemy's squadron in Aix Roads, 11th April 1809; and at the attempt made by Captain Malcolm to destroy two frigates, under the batteries of Cape La Hogue, and in November 1810 we subsequently find him serving on board the *San Joseph 110,* bearing the flag of Lord Keith, Commander-in-Chief of the Channel fleet. His first commission, whereby he was appointed a lieutenant of the *Impetueux 78,* flagship of Vice-Admiral (later Sir George) Martin, on the Lisbon station, bears date 14th August 1812.

Lieutenant Randolph's next appointment was 13th May 1813 to the *Eurotas* frigate, Captain (later Sir John) Phillimore, whom he 'ably assisted' in the gallant and hardfought action between that ship and *La Clorinde,* of 44 guns, 25th February 1814. In consequence of the dangerous wounds received by Captain Phillimore, the *Eurotas* was afterwards commanded, *pro tempore,* by Captains Edmund S. P. Knox and Robert Bloye, and ultimately by Captain James Lillicrap, under whom Lt. Randolph continued to serve till promoted to the rank of Commander, 13th June 1815. On 26th January 1819 he was appointed to the *Pandora* sloop, fitting out for the Irish station, which vessel he paid off in June 1822. His commission as Captain bears date 20th April 1827. He was later promoted on half pay to Rear Admiral on 13th July 1854, Vice Admiral on 7th November 1860 and Admiral on 15th June 1864. Most of this information comes from *Naval Biography*, Marshall, 1831.

We had an interesting day in Greenwich for, returning to St Alphage's Church, the burial place of General Wolfe and Thomas Tallis who was the organist there, we spent some time with the elderly verger examining the records and getting a few new Lambarde facts. Of course William Lambarde and other members of the family are also buried here. We looked at the Almshouses founded by William Lambarde as the College of Queen Elizabeth in 1576. They were rebuilt in 1819 by the Drapers' Company (Master Sir Thomas Plumer, Master of the Rolls) to whom William Lambarde gave the Lambarde Cup in 1577/78 which cost him at least £10, and which I believe they still possess. And what a remarkable coincidence that Wolfe's statue in Greenwich Park should overlook the site of Thomas Lambarde's first house at Westcombe whilst the Wolfe statue in Westerham is within earshot almost of his second house at Squerryes.

Captain Randolph, RN, married on 19th November 1829 his cousin Juliana Lambarde, the younger sister of the two Miss Lambardes seen by Miss Edwards walking with the Duchess of Dorset. About this time Multon Lambarde had sold Sevenoaks Park before which he had built a new rather rambling house at Beechmont about a mile to the south on the edge of the escarpment with a spectacular outlook over the Weald. It is possible that most of the alterations already mentioned at Great Comp date from this same period, for the house was soon to be occupied by Lambardes, for the first time we can be certain of. It is indeed quite probable that the tenancy of the Comp Estate was part of the marriage settlement, and as Multon was apparently well off he would be expected to bring Great Comp up to a standard fit for his daughter and a distinguished young naval officer. However, it is also possible that the Randolphs did not go to Great Comp until 1841 for in that year Multon Lambarde's son William who then owned Beechmont made a mortgage with Charles Grenville Randolph and Juliana his wife and the Rev. T. Randolph, who was Charles's elder brother, Rector of Much with Little Hadham, Hertfordshire. Of course the Randolphs may have been borrowing money to carry out their own building.

What is certain if my calculations are correct is that William Lambarde on 25th October 1842, the date of the Tithe Apportionment, owned the following land at Comp and Platt:

	Occupier	Acres	Roods	Perches	Description
Wrotham Parish	C. G. Randolph	150	3	22	Great Comp
		52	1	20	Potters Hole
	W. Lambarde			2	2 Tenements
	William Carter	10	2	24	Land on which Platt church and vicarage now stand
	C. G. Randolph			31	Lodge and Garden (Seers Cottage)
	William Carter	2	3	19	Jerrett Field
	C. G. Randolph	63	—	1	Eight pieces of land near Wrotham Nappson south of Maidstone-Sevenoaks Turnpike
		279	3	39	
Leybourne Parish	C. G. Randolph	16	1	18	Great Comp
	Francis Woodger	79	2	19	Little Comp
		95	3	37	
	Total	375	3	36	

Jerrett Field is the Suett of 1750 and 1631. Potters Hole must include High Heath (High Haught). In Leybourne parish Middle Comp Farm of 35 acres 2 roods 3 perches was occupied by W. Herrington of which 22 acres 3 roods 10 perches south of Comp Lane were owned by Henry Hughes and 12 acres 2 roods 33 perches north of Comp Lane were part of the Leybourne Glebe.

So in 1842 the Lambarde estate of 376 acres consisted of land in Platt and Platt Woods and Great Comp and Little Comp separated from each other by the wedge of Mid Comp just as they had always been separated by the Glebe (map page 143), the part south of Comp Lane having been acquired by Henry Hughes or his predecessors.

The Tithe Map of 1842 indicated distinctly all our present outbuildings, the terrace and walls of the square, the forecourt, but the extension we call Great Comp Cottage had not been built. Next door there are the barn, the cart shed, the shed and an oast with only one roundel, so the second must have been built later. The limes on each side of the drive appear to have been planted after the date of this map.

Captain Randolph, as he then was, was the first churchwarden of Platt Church which was built in 1841–42. Before that Great Comp was in Wrotham (except the part of the farm which was a detached part of Leybourne) of which the rector and vicar since 1805 was the Rev. George Moore. He it was who

A MAP of *Little Comp*
lying in the Parish of *Laborne* in KENT

North

South

Wrotham Walk

Smith

Late Walton Esq.

Tho. Chapman

Clark

Mr. Smith

Sts. Bartholomews

Harper

Tomlin

Cony C...

Cotton field
4 . 0 . 34

Hop garth

John Townsend

Three acre
2 . 2 . 0

...m field
3 . 37

Star Croft
2 . 3 . 3

2 . 3 . 20

Brambly ...

A R P
6 . 0 . 0

A R P
5 . 1 . 14

Bottom field
3 40

Barn field
3 . 3 . 23

Tovel field
3 . 2 . 10

Reeds
6 . 0 . 29

House field

Squire field
2 . 3 . 34

Great Broom f...
8 . 3 . 31

Little Broom f...

Pond field
4 . 3 . 0

2 . 2 . 15

Old Hop garn
7 . 0 . 14

PART OF LABORNE

Little Thirgoos

Newmans

Road to Offham

GREAT
COMP

Herods

GLEBE

during a riot in the hard times of the 1830s when surrounded in his rectory by 500 labourers crying 'bread or blood' and demanding that he halved his tithes as it was impossible for the farmers to pay them said 'he'd rather be hanged on the nearest tree than accede to such violent proceedings'. It is interesting to note in this connection that at Christmas 1835 Multon Lambarde caused two years' payment, ie £10 of Dodge's charity to be distributed indiscriminately amongst all the poor of the parish above 1,000 in number, and the same mode of distribution had been adopted in former years, two, three or four years' payments having been disposed of at one time instead of distributing the sum of five pounds every year amongst the more industrious of the poor selected for that purpose. The number of 1,000 seems extraordinarily large and must surely include just about all the working class and their families. We like keeping this charity going and still pay half of the five pounds to the vicar, having resisted a move to capitalise it. By 1843 Mr Moore had been a parson for nearly 50 years (died 1846) and perhaps he felt it was time to lessen his responsibilities. Platt parish was formed out of the hamlets of Platt, Crouch, Great Comp, Wrotham Heath and Nepicar formerly all part of the parish of Wrotham. But for some reason Great Comp house itself and farm was still left in the parish of Wrotham. The land for the new church was given by the Lambardes. The first parish priest was the Rev. John Mickleburgh, curate in charge, who became vicar of St Mary's when it was officially declared a parish church in 1846. He was a friend of the Randolphs and, as noted in his diary, often visited them at Great Comp. Unfortunately all the early parish records have been lost, but although Jane died in 1817 one can imagine some Austen-like gatherings at Great Comp to discuss the new church and other matters – William Lambarde and his wife Harriet, descended from King Alfred the Great, sister Mary and the Rev. Richard Solway, Captain Randolph and Juliana and the Rev. Thomas Randolph, the Rev. John Moore and Rev. John Mickleburgh; then there was Col. Richard Austen, himself of Jane's family who owned land at Crouch adjoining the Lambardes in Platt, not to mention the Hon. William Nevill, vicar of Birling, later fourth Earl of Abergavenny and a friend of the Randolphs. To add the essential romantic element William Lambarde had several young sons including William, Lieutenant RN, but I cannot find any girls of the right age, the vicar of Birling's three daughters being rather young. Jane Austen herself had two brothers who became admirals and who would no doubt have known Captain Randolph. All very fine, but I think the old house would hardly have provided a grand enough setting. All the same, partly to commemorate those times, we thought it appropriate to acquire five of the original pews when Platt Church was refurbished in 1979, and they are now in our tea room and elsewhere.

On another of our investigatory trips, this time on an overcast day with a bitter east wind, having been to the Archives office in Maidstone we thought we would have a look at Birling Manor, the ancient seat of the Nevills. Here if anywhere Ichabod is the word, as all we could see was a gate lodge, the remains of an imposing entrance gate and a carriage entrance to the church. Presumably the Rev. the Hon. William used both on his journeys to his church. The lady of the gatehouse enlightened us to the effect that Birling Manor was destroyed by fire during the First World War, and there was not a brick left. On such a day we found it a strangely moving experience. In the church itself we saw again but with much more personal interest the tall elaborately carved font cover presented in 1853 by the three daughters of the 4th Earl of Abergavenny (vicar here from 1817–44). It is quite remarkable that they did the actual carving, and you can see the initials of all three of them. The eldest, Caroline Emily, born in 1829 eventually became the owner of Great Comp. She was the goddaughter of Admiral Randolph, and while the Randolphs were at Great Comp they had land in Platt Woods cleared and planted with conifers and rhododendrons in preparation for a house it was planned to build for Lady Caroline as she had then become. The plan did not materialise and a hundred years later we were pleased to contribute five pounds very shortly after we came here towards the purchase of 40 acres of this same wood for the people of Platt for ever. The price was I believe about £1,500 (the value of the timber) of which the Malling Rural District Council paid half. Never shall we forget the public meeting arranged at short notice on 7th May 1959 at which almost the whole sum was collected by the end of the evening. This is where Thomas Lambarde in 1718 required a right of passage from Isaac Tomlyn.

Between Admiral Randolph's death at Great Comp in 1871 and his wife's in 1876 there were several indentures including a very elaborate one of 22nd August 1874 between Thomas Randolph of the first part and six other parties including Milton Lambarde three times (presumably William's son Multon), two of his brothers-in-law, R. W. B. Battiscombe and J. C. Trail, his sister Harriet Elizabeth, Juliana Randolph, three people called Holcroft, Lady Caroline Nevill and her sister Lady Henrietta Augusta Mostyn. Evidently arrangements were being made by Lady Nevill to acquire the estate and she appears to have mortgaged it for £20,000 to part of the one-third share of the residual estate of her father (ie left to the three sisters on trust). The deed of mortgage was dated 8th October 1874 and the mortgagees would be the trustees R. M. Leeke and Sir W. B. Riddell. So Lady Caroline owned Great Comp before the death of Juliana in 1876, but there is some doubt as to whether she ever occupied the house. At any rate the long ownership of the Lambardes, nearly 200 years, was over. In Sevenoaks Multon Lambarde bought the Bradbourne estate before he died on 21st December 1896 and his son Major William Gore Lambarde lived there, Beechmont becoming a preparatory school in 1905. The Major and his lovely Irish wife were keen and expert horsemen and his four-in-hand coach, himself handling the reins, was an appreciated sight in the town. He was still 'of Beechmont' after he sold Bradbourne in 1930. His brother, the seventh and last Multon, had died in 1882. William Gore Lambarde had a cousin, Brigadier-General Francis Fane Lambarde, and the latter's brother John Barrett Lambarde, died in 1957 (the year we came here) and is commemorated on a tablet in Sevenoaks Church 'last of his name'. So the Lambarde male line ended with two of the last three bearing names of the twins who died in the early 17th century; and still harping back, one of William Gore's two daughters, Mrs S. F. Campbell, was christened Deborah Sylvestre Fane after one twin and his mother. Was there a premonition that the line was coming to an end? Mrs S. F. Campbell died on 5th June 1976 which in fact did bring to an end the direct line of Lambardes.

Beechmont was destroyed by a flying bomb and the site was acquired from

Mrs Campbell by Mr and Mrs John Dunlop. Mr Dunlop is the son of Sir John whose book has been so useful to us. We have many times enjoyed the Sevenoaks Music Club informal concerts and Annual Meetings in the Dunlops' new Saltarium there, and the garden which they have so cleverly resuscitated and developed, without ever knowing its connection with Great Comp.

Coming back to Great Comp, in 1883 some land was sold enabling the mortgage to be reduced to £16,000, but exactly a year later on 26th October 1884 a further charge on the unsold portion increased the sum to £24,000. Between 1842 and 1905 William or Multon Lambarde or the Nevills acquired the 23 acres of Mid Comp perhaps from Henry Hughes, and the Little Comp land east of the Seven Mile Lane was sold to Viscount Falmouth, quite probably the 1883 transaction. The remainder of Little Comp west of the Seven Mile Lane and the fields Newmans and Little Thurgoes of the 1750 map were then added to Mid Comp to bring it to about 82 acres. Lady Nevill died unmarried on 23rd February 1887 and left the estate to her brother, the Hon. Ralph Pelham Nevill, DL, JP, of Birling Manor entailed to his male descendants. He was the only brother of the fifth Earl and first Marquess of Abergavenny, was much involved in county affairs, and High Sheriff in 1896, four years after Multon Lambarde held the same appointment.

The house appears to have been let throughout the Nevill ownership, but the following list of occupiers is not necessarily complete:

1874	Mrs Hall	1891	Henry G. Phelps
1882	John Court	1899	Capt. Henry Wetherall
	Rev, Thomas Shipden	1903	Patrick H. Maxwell, Farmer.
1887	ditto		

Captain Wetherall, who was one of the Churchwardens, left in October 1899. Mr Phelps could have been a son of Henry D. Phelps, Vicar of Birling, who died in 1864, aged 52.

The elder of the Hon. Ralph Nevill's two sons died in 1902, and after disentailment in 1904 he and his younger son Percy Llewellen Nevill sold Great Comp on 21st January 1905 to Mr Heron Maxwell for £8,000. The sale included 120 acres of Great Comp, 83 acres of Middle Comp and 41 acres of woods etc in hand, a total of $243\frac{1}{2}$ acres, and obviously the smaller part of the whole estate which was presumably worth £24,000, although it is difficult to see how it could have been. The Hon. Ralph Pelham Nevill died in 1919, a few years after he had seen the house he had lived in for more than 80 years burnt down.

Harry Lauder's Walking Stick, *Corylus avellana* 'Contorta'

A curious form of the Japanese larch *Larix kaempferi*

The Pope's urn framed by the upright
growing *Fagus sylvatica* 'Dawick' on the left,
and *Acer x lobelii* on the right, and the fine
old-rose 'Albertine'

Above: The Chilstone Temple with *Pyrus salicifolia* 'Pendula' on the right. The large oak in the background is just beyond the end of our garden

Below: The yew hedges and tea terrace and *Magnolia soulangiana* in May

Above: The nearest thing to perfect ground cover. *Geranium macrorrhizum* 'Ingwersen's Variety', with azaleas and our favourite *Viburnum* 'Lanarth'

Below: *Prunus pissardii, Pyrus salicifolia* 'Pendula' *Fagus sylvatica* 'Dawick' framing *Acer* 'Prinz Handjery'. In front of the Ribbon vase is one of the best golden yews, *Taxus baccata* 'Semperaurea'

The XXth century

We have a framed undated photograph of the house as it probably looked for much of the 19th century. The chickens running on the rough grass and general appearance of well-being are suggestive of a gentleman farmer not very interested in gardening. All this changed with the arrival in 1903 of Mr and Mrs Patrick Heron Maxwell first as tenants and then as owners. They came from Scotland and brought at least two 'retainers' as proved by the inscription pencilled on the inside of the wooden lining of one of the lead cisterns of the valve W.C.s that we demolished:

> James Geddes gardener from Duncree Scotland came to Great Comp 1904 and hopes to be able to make his fortune amongst the Kentish Hogs A-Men so let it Be.

> I hope to be home in time for Christmas amen Ch. Walsh Plumber December 1904 Newton Stewart NB I lined this cistern on Sunday for which I hope will not be a great sin.

We have moved from the world of Jane Austen and Dickens to that of Kipling, Jekyll and Siegfried Sassoon, a time when

> Uninterrupted cricket seasons were to come
> Beanfields were good to smell, and bees would always hum
> Kent was all sleepy villages, through which I went
> Carrying my cricket bag.

also a time

> While better men than we go out and
>   start their working lives
> At grubbing weeds from gravel paths
>   with broken dinner-knives.

It was the age of Edward VII and the Entente Cordiale and of Mrs Pankhurst and Lloyd George. It included both the zenith of the British Empire and the rise of Lenin, Trotsky and Stalin. And if I were asked to sum up the Maxwells' time at Great Comp I would say it was the Age of the Craftsman. It is not unnatural for me to think of Mrs Maxwell and Gertrude Jekyll (1843–1932), her near contemporary, especially but not exclusively in the context of gardening, but they were really very different. Miss Jekyll was a woman of culture and, dare I say it, taste, and an innovator, none of which I can see to any great extent in either of the Maxwells, but rather an overwhelming desire for order and excellence in everything they touched, and for someone with such a philosophy what a remarkable person Mrs Maxwell must have been to have involved herself in so many and so varied activities. Reading in the *West Kent W.I. News* the tributes to her from no fewer than five colleagues I see a woman who combined great powers of leadership with infinite attention to detail. I note words like kind, appreciative, courtesy, hospitality, punctiliousness, and shared knowledge. I also note that she was called Max by her friends and never Frances or Jane, and that 'It was Mrs Maxwell who questioned any ambiguity in the Minutes or pulled us up if we were out of order.' (Miss V. G. Thompson) – and she was a member of that committee for 32 out of its 37 years (West Kent Federation of Women's Institutes, County Executive). So with her 'strong character moulded by many vicissitudes of life' it is also not surprising perhaps that, for some, her memory is honoured well on this side of idolatry.

Mrs Maxwell was a prominent suffragist, president of both the Women's Cricket and the All-England Women's Hockey Associations, first chairman of West Kent Federation Women's Institutes, served on the W.I. National Executive Committee from its beginning until 1926, was chairman of its Handicrafts Subcommittee, founded with her friend Miss Mary Somerville the Guild of Learners of Handicrafts, and was Vice-Chairman of the Kent Women's Land Army from 1939 to 1945.

All this was reflected in her life at Great Comp. She was a skilled potter with her own kiln, and encouraged many other crafts like spinning, weaving, bee keeping, basketry and photography, and even as late as 1956 on our very first visit we found Miss L. M. Harris at the door of the Oasts in the process of turning out and dusting weaving equipment for use elsewhere. At this point it is worth noting that Joy said to me, 'If Miss Harris can live alone in the Oasts, so can I be alone in Great Comp when you have to be away for a night or two.' Mrs Maxwell played hockey for Kent and cricket and had cricket and hockey grounds laid out and a pavilion built which were used by county and national teams and teams from all over the world. The pavilion is now a house. She founded and played for the Pilgrims, a well-known women's hockey team which toured all over Britain. She produced and acted in plays here and elsewhere including an open air performance of *A Midsummer Night's Dream*, with her companion Miss Vera Cox who was also a fine hockey player. Further afield she ran a flower shop in London, sang in the Bach Choir, and practised her greatest hobby (*sic*) of mountain climbing in Switzerland every year.

In addition to all this Mr and Mrs Maxwell were building up a pedigree herd of Guernsey cattle and with three gardeners they made a garden of which in its heyday we have little record. From what we have seen and heard it was indeed very fine. The few photographs we have found must suffice.

Soon after they came to Great Comp the oasts, which had not been used for some time, were converted to a country cottage, and used by their friends Mr and Mrs McLaren mainly at weekends. During the First World War Mrs Maxwell helped to organise the Women's Land Army in Kent and Great Comp was a training centre where girls came to learn dairy work. According to Mr Fishenden there was a herd of goats during the war for cheesemaking.

Mr Maxwell sold most of Mid Comp Farm (less Comp Corner and half an acre) to Richard John Lane on 1st May 1922 leaving 162½ acres. He died on 14th January 1936 leaving the estate to his wife.

The Second World War made a big difference to the farm which was nearly all pasture except for a small acreage for growing food for the cows, as the grass was then ploughed up for growing corn and potatoes and the herd was dispersed. Tractors came to plough the first time, but after that their own two horses kept it going. The Pavilion was taken over for a Land Army store, part of The Oasts was used as a Land Army H.Q., and Land Girls came to work on the farm from Crouch House which was used as a hostel. The Crouch House that was demolished in 1968 was a Victorian building, though some timbers from a much older house were found in the interior which would be the old seat of the Millers.

Tea on The Oasts lawn. Mr Maxwell on the
left and Mrs Maxwell on the right

After the war things could hardly be the same and Mrs Maxwell was then over 80. But she carried on much as before but on a reduced scale, and on 16th October 1953 sold 12½ acres on the northeast and east of the present garden to Mr R. J. Ellingham, who had bought Mid Comp from Mr Lane. She had also let on the 29th September 1953, to Mr Ellingham, most of the arable land, about 72½ acres, for a rent of £200 per annum, which is interesting, as it is exactly the same rent that Dame Sarah Howell got from Edward Howell als Lucke for more than 630 acres in 1641. She did not retire from the W.I. County Committee until 1954, and in her last speech at the Annual Meeting she told them, 'In my ninety-first year I say to you we must always go on learning.' That year she did not feel up to the journey, but she missed the mountains so much that the following year she determined to go, and would try flying. A fortnight before she flew to Switzerland she was telling a colleague all her plans for future inter-county handicraft shows. After ten happy days her zest for gentians required her to take a trip in a chair lift. It proved too much for her heart and she died in Engeried Hospital, Berne, on 5th July 1955.

Mrs Maxwell left the estate to Miss Vera Cox who decided not to retain it, and the executors sold it on 20th September 1956 to Mr Edward R. Moulton-Barrett.

Mr Moulton-Barrett, the son of the late Lt. Col. Edward F. Moulton-Barrett, OBE, MC, of the Royal West Kent Regiment is not from Kent, but has spent much of his life within 15 miles of Great Comp. One of his forebears was an officer in the expedition which seized Jamaica from the Spanish in 1655 and from then on till quite recently the family remained in the Island as estate owners. One of his best known ancestors who was born in Jamaica was Edward Barrett Moulton-Barrett, generally referred to as 'Mr Barrett of Wimpole Street',

151

whose sister was Sarah Moulton the original of Sir Thomas Lawrence's famous portrait 'Pinkie'. His daughter who was a much admired poet in her own right became Elizabeth Barrett Browning, and her romantic marriage to Robert Browning formed the subject matter of Rudolph Bessier's play *The Barretts of Wimpole Street*. It was because Dennis Stanfield, Mr Moulton-Barrett's half brother who lived nearly all his adult life in Nigeria, wished to retire and live at Great Comp or the Oasts, that Mr Moulton-Barrett negotiated the purchase of the estate, and then on the same day resold the leased part to Mr Ellingham leaving 77½ acres. On 1st February 1957 Mr Moulton-Barrett sold Great Comp with 4½ acres of land to the rather unlikely present owners. He converted the barn to a house in 1960 for himself where he still lives.

Who were we to intrude on this scene? I think of the Nicolsons and the army. 'The military arrived at Sissinghurst. It consisted of the Headquarters of a Tank Brigade on exercise, heralded by a young officer of the name of Rubinstein . . . I was most polite to Captain Rubinstein . . .', and later referring to the Brigadier, 'He was a nice well-behaved man . . .'. Now, about that time, I had just been involved in several army moves including one from Scotland to Hothfield Common in Kent. What if it had been Sissinghurst and it had been Lt. Cameron of 664 Artisan Works Company, RE instead of a Tank Brigade? I hope they would have been polite in a kindly way, but I can imagine a diary entry 'bedint' or even worse. And here were we at least putting a foot into their world in 1957. Lady Nicolson undoubtedly knew Mrs Maxwell well, as both were on the Kent Land Army Committee, and she actually wrote a poem about Max on the latter's retirement from the County W.I. Committee:-

> Dear Max, there are several Maxes,
> There's Beaverbrook, Beerbohm and Co.,
> There are candles that gutter in waxes,
> There are papers that come for the taxes,
> But only one Max that we know.
>
> The one Max that never relaxes
> In the thousands of stitch she may sew;
> The Max that scales mountains with axes
> And tramples her boots in the snow.
>
> Grand Max, it is here we salute you
> And here that we send you our love.
> You have served and we cannot depute you
> To an Institute heaven-above.
>
> We would fain keep you here to befriend you
> As you have befriended our ranks,
> But since you resign we must send you
> Our love, our respect, and our thanks.
>
> (Signed) V.S-W.

This was the Sissinghurst Women's Institute contribution to the book presented to Mrs Heron Maxwell on her retirement from the Executive Committee of the West Kent Federation, W.I.

Later as one of the 'shillingses' we had a few words with Lady Nicolson at Sissinghurst, and were diffident enough not to mention that we were now at Great Comp. We had seen at Sissinghurst many plants which we had not seen anywhere except here, and we believe they often exchanged plants, including our ubiquitous *Campanula lactiflora.*

For better or worse we were now the owners of the main house of an estate which was at its peak at the start of the Civil War with over 630 acres, and was now down to 4½. This was its nadir, for our acquisitions of 1962 and 1975 have brought the acreage up to seven. But most of the original estate is still farmed as it has been for hundreds of years. When Mr Ellingham sold Mid Comp Farm in 1962, Mr F. G. Pierce now, in 1980, 85 years of age, bought most of it, and his sons William and Richard, now own and farm hundreds of acres including the beanfield between us and them along our northeast boundary. Mr and Mrs W. Chaplin on the land along our southeast boundary grow many fruit and vegetable crops, and were among the pioneers of self-picking. Customers, often whole families, come from Kent and the London suburbs, and from the large car park make their way home along a farm road which follows our southeast and then northeast boundaries to Comp Lane.

One of our garden visitors on 5th July 1980 said his name was Knight, and that in 1908 when he was five he was living at Little Comp where his father worked for Mr Pierce. When he and his wife were having tea he said to my wife, 'I used to come for milk somewhere about here'. – It was the very spot he was standing on. He used to walk to the school at Mereworth (2½ miles), sometimes getting a lift from the carrier, and remembers Mr Pierce's sons, Fred and Bill, as men in their twenties. My wife asked him if he knew anything of the Chapel remains, and she got quite excited when he said he remembered a tin hut which was used for services at that time.

In fact, our friend Mr Fred Pierce who had tea with us on 8th July was only 13 then (and had also walked to Mereworth school), and he could remember Mr Knight's father who he thought was his father's foreman. Mr Pierce said that the Maxwells never farmed Mid Comp themselves, but had let it to Mr Galloway, son of the owner of Mereworth Lawn, and then to Mr Sedgewick for a few years before selling it to Mr Lane. He confirmed that the Leybourne parson used to take services in Lent in the tin hut which Mr Pierce demolished before 1939. He remembered Mr Heron Maxwell as a gentlemanly man, never cross with anyone, recalled how he used to come with the laundry to Little Comp by pony and trap once a week, and return later to collect it – The Laundry was the present Comp Corner. The public footpath, through Thomas Lambarde's High Heath and conduit bank, was the Maxwells' private path to Platt Church, and trespassers were not encouraged. Mr Pierce also confirmed that the Fishendens' old house, Gate Cottage, was built by the Maxwells and that part of the fine central chimney had been damaged during the last war by a British plane out of control which crashed, killing the pilot, in the field to the west.

The Woodgers were tenants of Little Comp from *c.* 1780–1880. The widow of the 1842 Francis continued until 1875, then her son until he died in 1880, and in 1895 Little Comp was let to Mr Pierce's father William who had come from Marden and married a relation of these Woodgers. He subsequently rented the adjacent farm, Highlands, immediately after Viscount Falmouth had acquired it from a Mr Howard, moved there with his family, and later bought both farms from Viscount Falmouth. He died in 1949 aged 80. We much enjoyed talking to

Mr Pierce, a man who with his father built up an estate here and at Hadlow of about the same acreage as Sir John Howell's land in Kent, and we think the latter will be turning in his grave at the thought of the present turnover of the farm, even I think allowing for the debasement of the pound.

Two days later in the middle of the wettest and coldest July spell I can remember (49°F as I write at 6 p.m. – and how fortunate in a way for us to have little competition from the garden to take us away from the book), I went along to see Mr Frank Johns at March Cottage, Comp Lane, close to Comp Farm which is also known as Comp in the Hole. He is Chairman of the Offham Society, and supplied the following information from various sources:

The name Çomp is much more likely to be the Saxon field than either Hasted's or Fielding's suggestions. There is no evidence of Hasted's 'military way' and he also seems to have been mistaken in thinking the Iron Age Fort at Oldbury to have been Roman.

The detached part of Leybourne parish known as Comp was a hamlet of about 760 acres originally a den or swine pasture belonging to the Manor of Leybourne, and entirely covered by woodland as a large part of it is to this day. Sir Roger de Leybourne had acquired the land from Ralph Ruffyn and his bequest of glebeland to Leybourne Church was confirmed by his son Sir William in 1279. This glebeland was doubtless one of several clearances by the middle of the XIIIth century when a growing population brought about a land hunger, and which would later become the farms Comp, Little Comp, Great Comp, Glebe, Highlands and much later Mid Comp. Mr Johns considers Comp Farm nearest to Leybourne may have been the first to have been cleared and the earliest farm.

According to the 1634 terrier, the Glebe consisted of 115 acres, none of which could have been in Sir John Howell's estate, which accordingly must have extended further towards Wrotham than I had previously envisaged. The glebe terrier of the parish of Leybourne 1716 records 141 acres 'lying in Comp', $12\frac{1}{2}$ acres of which were south of Comp Lane. By Hasted's time it was about 130 acres, the $12\frac{1}{2}$ acres having been sold, confirmed by the Tithe Map of 1842, which also shows 432 acres were woodland out of a total acreage of 763. About 13 acres north of Comp Lane were occupied by W. Herrington and the rest was Glebe Farm. The Glebe is now 69 acres occupied by Wrotham Heath Golf Course – what a historical site for a Royal and Ancient game.

The Chapel of Ease of Leybourne which has entirely disappeared since Hasted's time, seems to have been in the field to the northwest of Comp Corner about 145 yards from the Seven Mile Lane and 90 yards from Comp Lane. It may have been abandoned after 1711 when the Rector of Leybourne lost a court action for tithes and woodland at Little Comp. The tin hut, in fact a brick building perhaps with a corrugated iron roof, may have started life as a farm cottage and was used later as a Toll House for the turnpike road from Wrotham Heath to Mereworth, the present Seven Mile Lane. Mrs Susan Bird was the toll collector in 1851 and by 1871 it was no longer used for the purpose, although Mr Pierce remembers the toll gates. The Seven Mile Lane was made c. 1795 after a Turnpike Act of that year. The conventional sign on the O.S. map (p.83) marks the site of the Toll House 'Chapel' and not, I think, the ancient chapel.

With Mr Johns I have tried to piece together the disposition of the roads and buildings at the Comp crossroads starting with Nicholas Miller's deed of 1606 and using the various maps, hoping that the house referred to in the deed is the one on the east side of the Seven Mile Lane and at right angles to it, the birthplace of Mr Fred Pierce. That house, however, is shown in its present position in both the 1750 and 1842 maps, whereas Nicholas Miller's was on the west side of the road. It could be the one shown there on the 1750 map, as the present house could well be of XVIIth century origin, extended later, part of which was Mr Maxwell's laundry, and which is now Comp Corner Cottage.

Over the period there have been obviously many major and minor changes to the roads making up the present Seven Mile Lane. Even allowing for possible inaccuracies in the maps – eg Hasted does not show any road whatsoever between Little Comp and Mereworth, whereas such a road would hardly have been allowed to disappear between 1750 and 1795 – it appears that the only section which has not been considerably realigned is that between Little Comp and Highlands. On the Tithe Map and also the 1819 Ordnance Survey, the present Highlands Farmhouse and Golf Clubhouse are marked Little Comp, which is strange, as Little Comp Farm has always been at Comp crossroads. In 1934 the 763 acres of the detached portion of Leybourne parish was transferred to Offham parish which was thereby more or less doubled in size.

Finally Mr and Mrs Jennings from Deal visited the garden and bought some plants. Mr Jennings was the Platt police constable and was present at the funeral of Mr Maxwell in 1936. He recalled the Maxwells' attempt to ensure the privacy of the path to the church which failed as their padlocked gate was broken down. He also remembered coming on Mrs Maxwell from behind and addressing her as 'Sir' which he continued to do when she turned and faced him.

Our garden and gardening make up the rest of the book, so to complete this little bit of history I will just include a few words about our Music Festival.

On Friday 28th June 1968 and Monday 1st July two garden parties were held here as part of the Golden Jubilee celebrations of the West Kent Federation, W.I. A large marquee was erected in the middle of the garden and a smaller one for a craft exhibition at the bottom. All that summer was unsettled and it would be impossible to think of more extreme conditions than on those two days, the first with pouring rain and a strong wind, both of which ceased as soon as the last guest had departed, and the second 80°F in the shade, blazing sun and a cloudless sky. I think it was on the Sunday that we decided to have lunch in the large marquee and thought how marvellous it would be if we could have a string quartet playing here for a private party.

Therefore when a few years later Clive Farahar, who was using our little dairy room (now the artists' room) for displaying old prints, wanted to entertain some friends and clients with a sherry party in the garden including music to be provided by his own small wind ensemble and the Purcell Club, a choir connected with Westminster School and Abbey of which he was the Secretary, we were not completely unprepared in our minds for what actually transpired. We felt it was too late in the year for an outside event so we hastily cleared out the stable which was choc-a-bloc with all the sort of things we can never throw away, cleared away the biggest of the cobwebs, collected as many chairs, stools, boxes and benches as we could muster, and the party duly took place on 23rd

September 1972. The guests sat facing the loft (which is now the gallery) and the artists ascended into the loft by means of a vertical ladder and narrow gangway.

It was a very fine concert followed by supper in the house, in fact it was so successful that we said to each other, 'We must do something with the stable'. One of our guests when writing to say thank you said, 'You must have a Festival'; which also set us thinking. We were not very keen on the word, but on consulting the dictionary we couldn't find a better. We had been members of the Sevenoaks Music Club for some years and Joy had been on the Committee, so with that experience and having asked a young pianist from Dunton Green, Bernard King, whom we had recently heard play at the Club if he could see concerts taking place in the stable, we decided then and there to proceed. We made a few alterations to the roof and loft, and were able to acquire 80 comfortable tip-up cinema seats from the Granada Organisation, and in September 1973 the first Great Comp Festival took place. Since then we have had so much pleasure from the music and other events even although tempered by the anxiety which is and always will be associated with the overall responsibility of running anything worth while, that it is almost invidious to mention any individuals. I think the remarkable fact that we celebrated Bernard King's 25th appearance on Saturday 10th September 1977 should be the exception. The first half of his programme exactly repeated his never-to-be-forgotten by anybody present first recital, but this time with no assistance from Jove, or should I say Donner. And what a privilege it was for us to have known and entertained the late Mr Vivian Langrish, so youthful and still teaching at the age of 86, and the late Mr Ben Travers equally so, still writing farces at the even greater age of 91. And how we used to look forward to the visits of the late Mr C. H. Gilbey. It was thanks to him (ignoring our request for some ornate carving) that we now possess such a good-looking concert Pleyel piano, so suitable for both the stable and our drawing room. He tuned it for many years and we shall never forget his visits on concert mornings when we used to enjoy his inexhaustible fund of anecdotes over a cup of tea or a glass of sherry.

Six years after the first concert the 131st event and 87th concert was given on 22nd September 1979 by the Chilingirian String Quartet (taking part for the sixth successive year) playing Beethoven's Quartet Op. 131 and Jennifer Ward Clarke playing, with them, the Schubert Quintet which has two cellos.

Many things go to make up the Great Comp Festival apart from the actual event, the garden, the weather, the stable, the bar, the flowers (and the evocative smell of the last three), the floodlighting, coffee afterwards, and a full and appreciative house. But what makes a concert a complete success is I think very personal, and another of life's mysteries, like what makes a memorable tune or quotation. We had been looking forward to this concert perhaps more than any other before, and even the weather was right. There was a full house, and the atmosphere in the crowded bar beforehand was perfect. The concert that followed can only be described in the words of one of our audience in her letter of thanks afterwards as 'sublime'. It is not too much to think that it was possibly the most perfect single event ever to happen here in our time and perhaps even throughout the long history of the house.

Above: The roaring fire in the middle room
Below: All ready for a piano recital in the stable

The Chilingirian String Quartet on 14th
September 1975 – our Silver Wedding

GREAT COMP FESTIVAL

1975

1979

Sunday, 14th September   8 p.m.

CHILINGIRIAN STRING QUARTET

Levon Chilingirian	—	Violin
Mark Butler	—	Violin
Simon Rowland-Jones	—	Viola
Philip de Groote	—	'Cello

Schubert   Op. 29 in A minor

Beethoven   Op. 130 in B flat to be played with its
original finale, Die Grosse Fuge

Tickets £2.50 (including coffee after the performance).

Saturday, 22nd September   8 p.m.

CHILINGIRIAN STRING QUARTET
with JENNIFER WARD CLARKE — 'Cello

Levon Chilingirian	—	Violin
Mark Butler	—	Violin
Nicholas Logie	—	Viola
Philip de Groote	—	'Cello

Quartet Op. 131 in C sharp min.   *Beethoven*
String Quintet in C   *Schubert*

Tickets £5.50 (including coffee after the performance).

A perfect Festival evening

A winter scene from the front porch. The silver birches
beyond Comp Lane make a striking background.

160

A tour round the Garden

We will walk round the garden following the numbers on the plan and I will mention only plants which are uncommon or of particular interest for their fruit, scent, autumn colour, etc. Some of our favourite plants such as phlox, lupins, philadelphus, azaleas, and also most of the smaller herbaceous plants hardly get a mention. Starting logically with (1), as you enter from the car park there are *Mahonias, japonica* and *lomarifolia*, and between them a hybrid of which they are the parents called 'Charity'. In front of them are *Skimmia japonica* 'Rubella', *Sarcococca humilis, Drimys lanceolata, Hypericum* 'Summer Gold' the prostrate *Polygala chamaebuxus,* some plants of *Ophiopogon planiscapus* 'Nigrescens', *Pieris* 'Forest Flame' and *Viburnum propinquum.* The evergreen *x Osmaria* 'Burkwoodii', the yellow-leaved *Weigela* 'Looymansii Aurea' and the small tree *Acer pseudoplatanus* 'Prinz Handjery' are underplanted with *Geranium macrorrhizum* 'Ingwersen's variety', *G. ibericum* and a clump of *Euphorbia griffithii* 'Fireglow'.

Coming forward into the front lawn (2) we pass a shrub you will see a lot of – *Viburnum plicatum* 'Lanarth' – and next to it *Paeonia lutea ludlowi.* There are several viburnums on the way up including *V. x carlcephalum, V. x hillieri* 'Winton', *V. harryanum* (with small circular leaves), a good form of *V. plicatum* (Japanese Snowball), behind it *V. henryi,* a compact berrying form of the guelder rose *V. opulus* 'Compactum' and nearer the front the small *V. farreri* 'Nanum'. Behind by the car park is *Carpinus betulus columnaris.* Also in the front of this bed are young plants of *Magnolia liliiflora* 'Nigra' and *Enkianthus chinensis.* Of the many herbaceous plants here *Viola cornuta* 'Alba' blooms all summer; others are *Gillenia trifoliata, Geum montana* (with fluffy seed heads), and *Viola* 'Maggie Mott'. As we stand on the bottom paving notice (3) the Erigeron round the curve of the lawn and the sword leaves of *Yucca filamentosa,* one on each side, and many self-sown *Sisyrinchium striatum.* Across the lawn the large grasses are *Stipa gigantea.* Overhanging the wall are several *Bolax glebaria* and at the far end of each wall is a young *Ginkgo biloba* and near the one on the right *Ostrya carpinifolia.* This area and the next are intended to have too many small plants to mention. Climbing the steps to the next paving note on the right a variegated form of *Yucca filamentosa* which we hope will prove to be hardy, and on the other side at the back *Rosa primula* with aromatic leaves. The two golden yews were grown from cuttings, probably *Taxus baccata* 'Aurea', and next to the one on the left are *Acer ginnala* and *Magnolia stellata* 'Water Lily'. On the way up the steps to the top terrace (4) on the left by the car park are *Sorbus hupehensis obtusa, S. rufo-ferruginea,* and *S. hupehensis* with pink berries, on the right is *S. cashmiriana* with white berries, and up at the top near the road *S. esserteauana.* At the foot of the wall on the right are *Iris pallida* 'Variegata', *Dictamnus fraxinella,* nerines and agapanthus. On the wall on the right are *Hebe* 'Bowles Hybrid', *Berberis empetrifolia* and seedlings of *Lavandula stoechas.* Shrubs on the way up are on the left the evergreen *Berberis veitchii* and behind it *B. francisci-ferdinandii, Corokia x virgata* and varieties of *Berberis thunbergii* 'Erecta', 'Aurea', 'Rose Glow' and 'Atropurpurea Nana'. On the right are several *Berberis thunbergii* 'Erecta' and

Rodgersia podophyllum with *Picea omorika* and *Metasequoia glyptostroboides* on the right background.

B. x stenophylla 'Corallina'. By the steps up to the top terrace are *Rosa ecae* with 'Zigeuner Knabe' behind (purple flowers and good hips), *Berberis verruculosa* one of a pair on each side – evergreen – and up by the road the evergreen *B. x lologensis*. The two cypresses are our own cuttings of *Chamaecyparis lawsoniana* 'Kilmacurragh'. In the little bed in front of the balustrade are *Myrtus communis tarentina, Ruta graveolens* 'Variegata' which often comes true from seed, *Fuchsia thymifolia* and *Abelia grandiflora*. On the right is the large sword-leaved *Phormium colensoi*.

Along the path parallel to the road are many Exbury azaleas grown from seed. The small tree on the left is *Ptelea trifoliata*, 'Hop Tree', with interesting and very long lasting seed heads, and then *Amelanchier asiatica* (here so far not attacked by birds). On the right we have passed *Cornus florida rubra, Decaisnea fargesii* (no blue pods yet), *Magnolia x proctoriana, Corylus avellana* 'Contorta' (twisted nut, Harry Lauder's walking stick, it's better in winter), *Magnolia* x 'Lennei', further in *Hydrangea bretschneideri* and near the path *Styrax obassia* (large round leaves). The tree heaths at the roadside are self-sown seedlings of *Erica arborea* 'Alpina' which we collected from the original ones on the old southeast boundary. Round the large stone seat (5) is *Hedera helix* 'Conglomerata'. Here are *Rosa farreri persetosa* (Threepennybit Rose), *Hydrangea* 'Preziosa' and behind it *Aronia arbutifolia* (autumn colour). Looking down the path, on the right are *Chionanthus virginicus* (Fringe Tree), *Magnolia* x 'Picture' and *Salix matsudana* 'Tortuosa' (Twisted Willow), and on the left a small *Stewartia pseudocamellia* and *Magnolia kobus borealis*. Proceeding along the top path you pass areas of the Irish heath *Daboecia cantabrica* mainly the variety 'Alba'. On the left is *Acer palmatum* 'Osakazuki', *Evodia hupehensis* (flowers in late summer), and *Embothrium coccineum* 'Norquinco Valley', underplanted with *Gaulthettya x wisleyensis* varieties of epimedium and *Veratrum nigrum*. On the right we have passed *Hamamelis japonica* 'Arborea', several *Clethra* spp, *Eucryphia* 'Nymansay', several plants of the charming little *Galax urceolata,* and round to the early flowering *Rhododendron* 'Elizabeth'.

We now reach the middle path from the main front lawn (6). A short walk back towards the lawn includes on the left the pink flowered *Magnolia x loebneri* 'Leonard Messel', behind it *Carya illinoensis* (Hickory), two *Acer capillipes* (snake bark), *Idesia polycarpa* (with large leaves), and coming back on the other side *Styrax japonica, Viburnum* 'Deben', *Rhododendron* 'Lady Chamberlain', *Magnolia x loebneri* 'Merrill', and back to *R.* 'Elizabeth'. The common birch, *Betula pendula,* in the middle of the path, turned out to have such a good bark that we left it there. To the right the tree with circular leaves is *Cercidiphyllum japonicum* and further in the remarkable variety of the Scots pine, *Pinus sylvestris* 'Aurea' (green in summer, bright yellow in winter). On either side of the bend in the path are two red oaks, *Quercus rubra*. On the right is *Nyssa sylvatica* and a *Magnolia x soulangiana,* our oldest layer from the 'Maxwell' one in the Yew Garden (23), and on the left at the back are two very fast growing small-leaved southern beech from Chile, *Nothofagus obliqua*. The Bird Cherry at the edge of the path is *Prunus padus* 'Albertii' (7). Looking along the path to the right is *Osmanthus delavayi, Hamamelis mollis* 'Pallida', and beyond the yellow pine is the *Acer negundo* 'Variegatum'. On the left is a

One of the best specimens anywhere of the
variety of the Californian Redwood
Sequoia sempervirens 'Cantab'

fine hornbeam *Carpinus betulus* 'Fastigiata'. Behind it is *Acer japonicum* 'Aureum' and so far the best of our *Hamamelis mollis*. At this corner there are several plants of the prostrate shrub *Lithospermum diffusum* 'Heavenly Blue'. Going down to the two large *Picea omorika* you pass on the right an interesting small rhododendron with blue leaves, *R. lepidostylum,* a mat of *Gaultheria procumbens,* with *Vaccinium glaucoalbum* growing in it. The large-leaved *Rhododendron falconeri* is in too open a position, behind it is a young *Arbutus menziesii* which will perhaps provide some shade in due course. Opposite the weeping yew is *Metasequoia glyptostroboides,* and another *Styrax obassia.*

We now leave the part of the garden which has been developed from the front field from 1959 onwards and come to the Doulton urn (8); which ends the vista from the summer-house (1).

Of the five paths take the outside one on the left which is in the strip of ground bought in 1962, and note five small trees, on the right *Acer rufinerve* and *Styrax hemsleyana;* on the left *Pterostyrax hispida, Acer griseum* with the peeling brown bark, and *Halesia monticola.* At the junction with the next path (9) there is a good *Skimmia japonica* 'Rubella' which has red buds throughout the winter, and highly scented flowers in the spring. Here the character of the garden has completely changed in two years following the removal of four large beech trees. Previously little but daffodils would grow in this part, now we have planted mainly heathers and conifers to take advantage of the open site. The 'ruins' were started before the removal of the beeches and completed(?) in late 1979. Continuing, on the right there is a collection of dwarf rhododendrons, then along the edge of the path several *Sarcococca humilis,* sweetly scented in early spring. Opposite, the large shrub with pinnate leaves is *Sorbaria arborea.* The two large cypresses were the only ones in the garden in 1957; just beyond them is a silver fir *Abies nordmanniana* which has only recently put on much growth, and on the opposite side is *Salix caerulea* (the cricket bat willow).

When we pass the multi-branched *Quercus ilex* (evergreen oak) (10) we are in the two acres bought in 1962 and in this area nothing is older than that year. We pass six Lombardy poplars *Populus nigra* 'Italica'. The area on the right is a good example of *Geranium* 'Claridge Druce' and other plants as complete ground cover. Near the seat at the east corner of the garden in front of the urn is *Osmaronia cerasiformis* (11). There are several Sorbus including along the path two whitebeams, *Sorbus aria* cultivars. On the right tucked in behind the laurel is the interesting early flowering *Sycopsis sinensis.* Apart from Scots pines the three conifers on the right are *Tsuga heterophylla* (Western Hemlock), *Abies grandis* and *Pinus ponderosa.* In the middle of the bed there is a large *Staphylea colchica.* And so we arrive at our best known view (12) of the heathers with the house in the background which we see from under the shade of the maple, *Acer saccharinum.* The tree to the right of the weeping willow and nearer to us is the autumn colouring *Liquidambar styraciflua* and there is a London plane, *Platanus x hispanica,* to the right of the three Scots pines. On the left in the middle distance the large bush is *Cotinus americanus* which last year was spectacular in flower, something like candy floss followed by several weeks of brilliant autumn colour, one of the best of all.

Continuing towards the temple there are several *Abies grandis* on the left and groups of ground-covering plants including *Sedum* 'Autumn Joy' with

Anaphalis triplinervis (a very good combination), *Polygonum amplexicaule* 'Atrosanguineum' (docklike leaves, flowers from the end of June until the frosts) and opposite the Rose of Sharon, *Hypericum calycinum*. Still on the left is the red horse chestnut, *Aesculus x carnea* 'Briotii', the manna ash, *Fraxinus ornus,* and in the middle of the path further on the Corsican pine, *Pinus nigra* (the varietal name has been queried in this case). The path was altered slightly when the temple was built, and the tree was too good to destroy. On the right we have passed *Pinus muricata,* Bishop's pine, which holds its cones for forty years, *Prunus serrula* (polished brown bark), and the spreading *P.* 'Tai Haku'' possibly the best single white flowering cherry. Ground cover plants here include *Symphytum grandiflorum* (dwarf comfrey) epimediums with *Hosta* 'Thomas Hogg', periwinkles and of course our old friend *Geranium macrorrhizum*. Beyond the pine in the path on the right is my wife's sycamore grown from a seedling, and a collection of some sixteen different species of viburnum including *V. betulifolium, V. hupehensis, V. lobophyllum, V. cassinoides, V. rhytidophyllum* and the evergeen *V. cinnamomifolium*. On both sides here are many plants of *Tellima grandiflora* 'Rubra'. Its good red leaves in the winter go well with *Viburnum x bodnantense* 'Dawn'. The weeping willow leaved pear, *Pyrus salicifolia,* and the monkey puzzle, *Araucaria araucana,* and several large azaleas we acquired with the ground in 1974. This is the temple garden (13) with the Chilstone Temple in the middle. At first we retained the original grass as a lawn round it, but in 1977 we decided to dig up the lawn and in its place keep the open character by planting a collection of hardy geraniums and other herbaceous plants. The large grass is the wild oat, *Stipa gigantea,* and the potentilla near the temple is a recent variety of *Potentilla fruticosa* with very bright yellow flowers called 'Goldfinger'. We planted a forsythia hedge along the new boundary in the knowledge that the birds would ensure that it would never be too much of a good thing. The very large oak at the end is not ours; it is estimated by some good judges to be no more than about 200 years old. We have now reached the end of the garden and will return by the other path curving towards the tallest of our *Abies grandis;* the other abies to the right was bought as *grandis* but is probably *concolor*. Back into the two acres at the junction of two paths note the small-leaved aromatic *Nothofagus antarctica* (14), and carrying straight on, on the right two red oaks, *Quercus coccinea* and *Q. palustris, Cryptomeria japonica* 'Elegans' and several *Holodiscus discolor* (like a spiraea). Opposite there is a clump of bamboo, *Arundinaria japonica,* then further back is a catalpa which was in the garden when we came, and further on a tulip tree which we planted and which has just started to produce a few blooms – *Liriodendron tulipifera*. Between the catalpa and the tulip tree there is a rampant *Polygonum baldschuanicum* on an old apple tree which we have to watch to stop it climbing into the nearby *Cornus kousa chinensis* and the yellow-leaved nut, *corylus avellana* 'Aurea'. On both sides of the path here are more Exbury azalea seedlings and the prostrate ground cover is *Ajuga reptans* 'Purpurea'.

Turn right (15) into our glade in which we are hoping to maintain a small collection of wild flowers presented by David McClintock (16). There are five young magnolias. *M. x soulangiana* 'Alba Superba', *M. officinalis, M. sieboldii, M. tripetala(?)* and *M. sargentiana robusta,* none of which have really

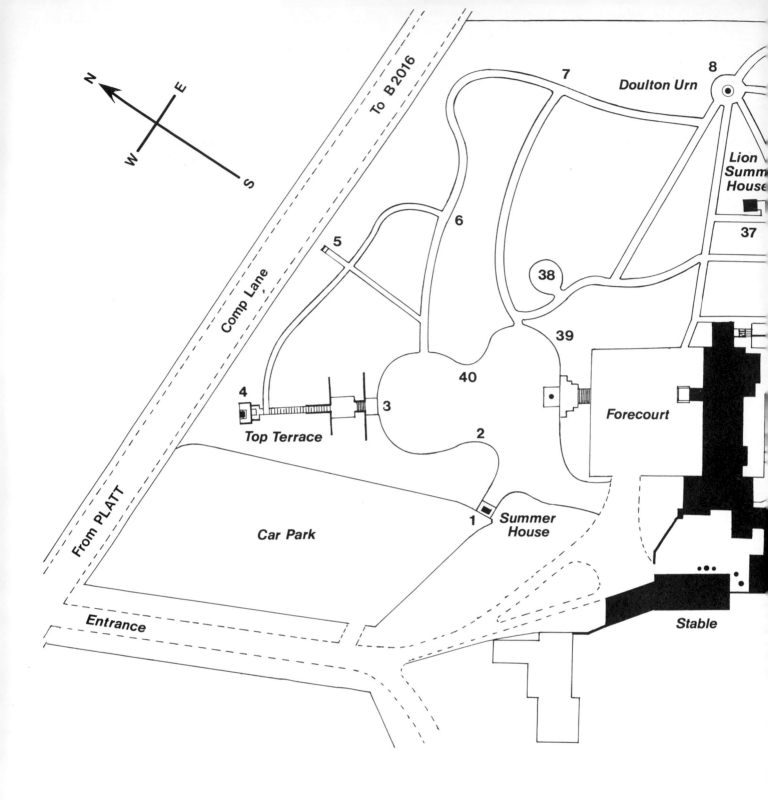

got going, but we have some hope. Behind the *Viburnum henryi* is the umbrella pine, *Sciadopitys verticillata*. The two large-leaved pines in the middle are *P. wallichiana* and *P. coulteri* which is reputed to have the largest cones of any pine. The herbaceous plant with the curious yellow bobbly flowers is *Phlomis russeliana*. Leaving the glade (17) look to the right at *Alnus incana* 'Aurea' which has red catkins and *Acer nikoense,* then turn left past the charming pink flowered *Viburnum plicatum* 'Pink Beauty', *Halesia carolina,* past a little bay of herbaceous plants and then note the Indian horse chestnut *Aesculus indica*

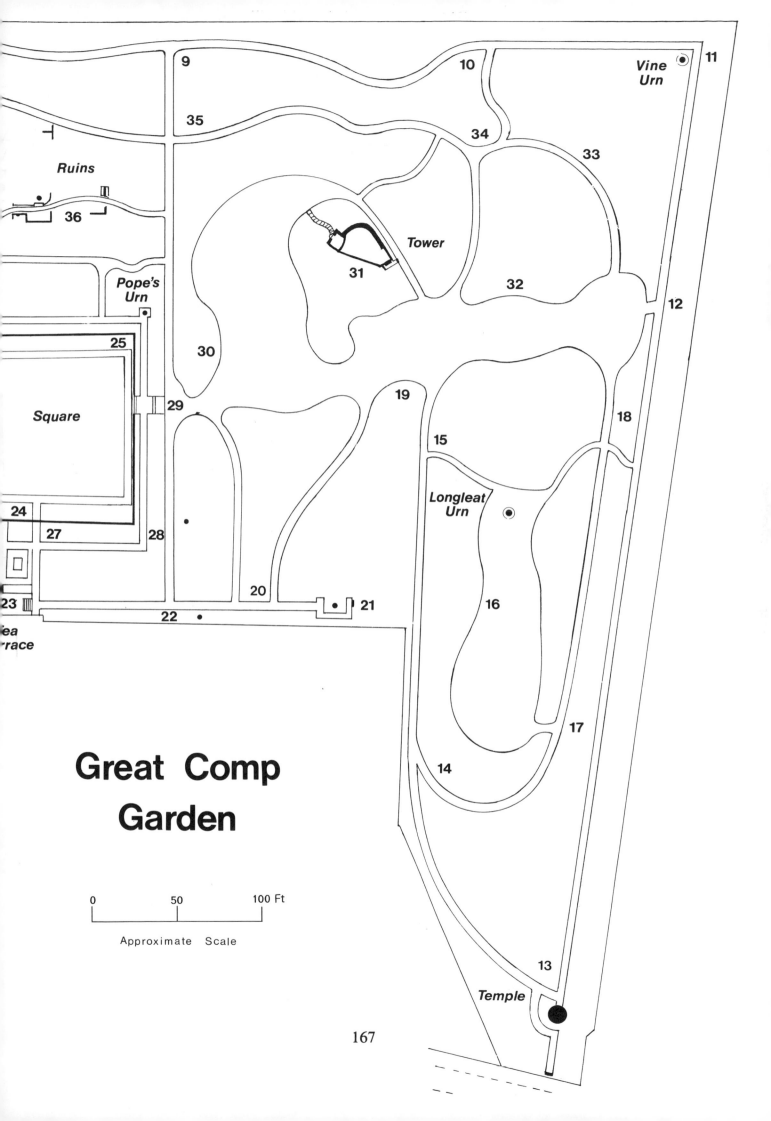

Great Comp Garden

9

10

Vine
Urn

11

35

34

33

Ruins

36

Tower

31

32

12

Pope's
Urn

30

25

29

Square

19

18

24

15

27

28

Longleat
Urn

20

16

23

ea
rrace

22

21

14

17

13

Temple

0   50   100 Ft

Approximate   Scale

167

which blooms later than the common one. There are one or two fine Christmas trees (*Picea abies*) hereabouts, some of which we hope to retain. Turning back into the glade between the Cedar of Lebanon, *Cedrus libani,* and *Crataegus crus-galli* note the curious narrow larch, one of three seedlings we bought of *Larix kaempferi,* and further on by the path the wild service tree, *Sorbus torminalis.* By the seat (18) there is a small collection of woodland plants, mainly hardy ferns and primroses. Going out of the glade notice the view of the tower through the heathers and the *Cedrus deodora,* and behind you the Longleat urn. Straight ahead (15) by the liriodendron is a clump of *Cornus alba* varieties 'Spaethii' and 'Elegantissima'. Turn right and note in the heathers the dwarf Scots pine *P. sylvestris* 'Beuvronensis' and in passing a close-up of *Cotinus americanus* on your left (19).

Back in the original four-and-a-half acres we come to the diagonal path with a good unnamed rhododendron seedling with oval leaves on the right. Of the conifers the large one in the middle is *Cryptomeria japonica* and further on *Picea brewerana.* On the left is *Acer cappadocicum,* and at the end (20) *Acer pseudoplatanus* 'Prinz Handjery' (similar to 'Brilliantissimum'). A little detour to the left past the very quick growing Turkey oak (*Quercus cerris*) brings you to a seat under the splendid old medlar (21), *Mespilus germanica.* We removed some of the paving here in 1977 and used it in the front garden. Carrying on towards the tea terrace there are several upright trees, botanically named fastigiate, planted to avoid branches hanging over our neighbour's garden, several varieties of Lawson's cypress, two Dawick beeches (*Fagus sylvatica* 'Fastigiata'), two oaks (*Quercus robur* 'Fastigiata') one on each side of the path, *Calocedrus decurrens* and the crab *Malus tschonoskii* which has brilliant early autumn colour. Near the Dawick beeches is a fastigiate form of golden yew (Taxus) (22). Looking towards the old beech area (9) in front of you the beds on each side have been emptied and left empty of herbaceous plants until we are sure that we have got rid of bindweed. Going on notice on the right a tall line of *Rosa rubrifolia* behind the azaleas – you will have seen many more in the garden – a unique rose for its coloured foliage and it also gives good hips in the autumn. All in the garden are seedlings from our original one. Behind the weeping birch, *Betula pendula* 'Youngii', is a fastigiate maple *Acer x lobelii.*

The Yew Garden (23) is our only home for hybrid tea roses round the little pond. The shrub by the tearoom door is a pomegranate, *Punica granatum* 'Flore Pleno'. The *Magnolia x soulangiana* was in the garden when we came. The yew hedge including the four tall columns is mostly more than 90 years old. Unfortunately coarse growing plants were used which are so vigorous that it really needs cutting twice a year instead of the one cutting I give it in August. It looks quite good, but we have seen much better elsewhere when finer-leaved slower growing plants were used. It was in such very poor condition when we came that we cut out a lot of it and planted several seedlings that we found in the garden. We also simplified the cutting by doing away with the castellations.

What we call the Square is entered through a circular arch (24) and shaded by a large *Eucalyptus gunnii* planted in 1961. Going round anti-clockwise beyond the *Viburnum plicatum* 'Rowallane' is the wonderfully scented but not too vigorous *Magnolia x watsonii* (one flower can scent half of the Square), and in the corner possibly the best golden yew, *Taxus baccata* 'Semperaurea', which is recovering after some shrubs which were overcrowding it have been removed. The evergreen tree at the opening with the brick steps is one of the most interesting trees in the garden, a form of *Sequoia sempervirens* which we bought from Hillier's in February 1961 as 'Nana Pendula'. It is now called 'Cantab' and far from being prostrate it produced a terminal leader straight away. How fortunate it is for us that it has not proved as vigorous in a prostrate direction. The mixed border is still not completely satisfactory because we have cleared a section at a time to get rid of bindweed, and it is a slow process. The pine (*Pinus bungeana*) (25) has white bark after a sufficient number of years. Of the shrubs behind the wall *Sorbaria aitchisonii* is in our opinion more elegant than the *S. arborea* already mentioned, and we find it less suckering. Beyond at the corner there is a group of shrubs (26) including *Osmanthus delavayi, Magnolia stellata, Buddleia* 'Lochinch', *Berberis calliantha* and under the *Magnolia grandiflora, Choisya ternata* (the Mexican orange). The two junipers below the house terrace are the spreading *J. x media* 'Pfitzerana Aurea'. These extremely vigorous shrubs are carefully pruned 'little and often', particularly the one at the steps. Beyond the steps are two more junipers, *J. communis* 'Hornibrookii' (prostrate) and the columnar 'Hibernica'. Between the house and the round arch are *Sorbus discolor* with good autumn colour, *Rhododendron* 'Blue Diamond' and *R.* 'Blue Tit', *Viburnum x burkwoodii* and *Hydrangea villosa*. There is also our best tree paeony, *P. lutea ludlowii*.

Through the arch (24) we turn left into an enclosed garden (27) which has not been satisfactory, possibly because of honey fungus, causing several losses including a good *Hamamelis mollis,* and the original *Magnolia grandiflora* which the older Mr Fishenden 'couldn't abear' because it never flowered. This would be because it was pruned back hard every year and not allowed to grow higher than the wall. We are pleased we managed to get a layer from it. In its place is a young *Azara serrata.* Next to it against the wall is *Carpenteria californica,* the climber *Actinidia chinensis, Syringa* 'Bellicent' and a very upright *Ginkgo biloba.* At the end (28) note the two good slender rich green cypresses, *C. lawsoniana* 'Kilmacurragh', planted in 1962. Between them is *Berberis verruculosa,* and the big architectural herbaceous plant is *Acanthus spinosus.* Take a seat for a minute and look at the Pope's Urn which is a replica of one in the poet's garden at Twickenham. Alexander Pope, one of the very greatest poets, said he was as interested in his garden as he was in writing poetry. The newly laid paving replaces an ash path with stone edges which was very difficult to maintain. On the left are shrub roses and herbaceous plants (and bindweed), and on the right predominantly evergreens. Note *Picea pungens* 'Globosa', *Chamaecyparis obtusa* 'Pygmaea', a cutting of ours of *Taxus baccata* 'Semperaurea', *Berberis calliantha, taxus baccata* 'Adpressa Variegata', *Pinus mugo,* and then flanking the new steps the pair of *Juniper x media* 'Pfitzerana' (29). But before you come to the junipers look over the parallel grass path to the old *Prunus* 'Pissardii' and to the right of it the *Cornus controversa,* an unusual tree with tiered branches. To the left of it across the far path the large leaved *Magnolia veitchii* planted in 1964.

To the left of the magnolia but nearer is *Cornus kousa* which produced in 1979 for the first time a magnificent display of its pink/white flower-like bracts. Turning right down the steps (29) we come to the main cross vista. Notice ahead the curious spiral branches of a *Thuja plicata*. A few yards along to the left note *Rosa x dupontii* on the left and *R.* 'Raubritter' on the right, with its unique pink globular flowers. Come back round our original heather bed (30) and note the well shaped cone of *Picea albertiana* 'Conica', and fairly near it the flattish *Abies balsamea* 'Hudsonia', two dwarf cypresses *C. lawsoniana* 'Minima Aurea', and *C. obtusa* 'Nana Gracilis', and an upright golden yew (our own cutting). All these plants are over 20 years old. The heathers at the sharp end are ordinary seedlings brought from the woods nearby and are over 20 years old having been pruned every year in April. The little group of *Calluna vulgaris,* 'H. E. Beale', a few feet away is also about 20 years old. Going round what we call the Crescent we come to a large *Viburnum* 'Lanarth', *Rhododendron* 'Unique' and *Rubus* 'Tridel' (a vigorous hybrid with large white flowers in May like a single rose). The two cherries were probably the last trees planted by Mrs Maxwell. The larger is the double Gean and the other is 'Ukon'. Looking across towards the Pope's urn is *Sorbus sargentiana,* a small tree remarkable for its bright red buds, large pinnate leaves, and one of the best of our trees for autumn colour. Past a *Sorbus hupehensis,* another *Cotinus americanus* and the smaller *Cotinus coggygria purpureus* are two *Eucryphias, glutinosa* and another form of *nymanensis* flowering a fortnight later than the one in front. We now come to our tower (31). As you go up the steps note on the left the low variety of the common laurel 'Otto Luyken'. At the platform note in the curve of the wall *Nandina domestica, Lippia citriodora* (Lemon Verbena), *Abelia grandiflora* and a good rosemary 'Benenden Blue'. Climbing further up you will get a good all-round view. The tree heaths, *Erica arborea* 'Alpina', were in the overgrown boundary when we came, and any others in the garden are seedlings from them. It is from the roots of *E. arborea* that briar pipes are made. Note the young self-sown oak seedlings which I am pruning to get them up on trunks.

Now we come down into the central 'sweep'. The old pond at the foot of the tower has become a small bog garden. Note two interesting plants, the large biennial Angelica whose stems can be crystallised and the thistle-like foliage and curious flower of *Morina longifolia.* The weeping willow was planted before we decided to have heathers there, but we think the combination is not as bad as one might have expected, and the Cornish heath seems to put up with it. Looking away from the house towards the maple there are groups of (32) *C. v.* 'Robert Chapman' with its bright red foliage in winter, large drifts of winter flowering *Erica x* 'Darley dale', *x* 'Silberschmelze', *E. carnea* 'Springwood White', *C. v.* 'J. H. Hamilton' and at the far end a mixed planting of *C. v.* 'H. E. Beale' and 'Peter Sparkes'. There are many more varieties on the other side, and about 200 varieties altogether in the whole garden. The broom behind them by the Scots pines is *Genista cinerea* which flowers in June and July and also the rather gaunt *G. aetnensis* flowering rather later, which we consider most elegant. Along the curving path on the left and right (33) are many fairly strong growing shrubs underplanted mainly with geraniums and hostas to give almost complete ground cover, with odd clumps of other plants such as phlox, and an interesting plant *Selinum tenuifolium* like a very ornamental cow parsley. There are also a number of hellebores including a good area of *H. corsicus*? seedlings. There are two young *Magnolias, wilsonii* on the left and 'Lennei' on the right.

The trees on the left beyond the larch are *Acer campestre, Quercus palustris* and *Quercus coccinea*. Behind are *Acer nikoense, Acer japonicum* 'Aureum' and a small *Catalpa bignonioides* 'Aurea' planted in 1964 and the larger *Acer rubrum*. On the right behind some *Rhododendron* 'Blue Diamond' (34) is a fine young *Magnolia salicifolia* planted in 1970 which flowered well for the first time in 1979. The evergreen oak to the right with choisya at its base is an unknown mistake, bought as *Quercus cerris*. Further on is a small plant of *Kalmia latifolia*. Opposite there used to be an enormous old hawthorn with nine trunks which I removed in the winter of 1971/72. Further up the slope on the left *Magnolia sieboldii* suffered severely in 1976 but is now recovering. Next are *Parrotia persica, Cornus florida rubra, Sorbus hybrida* 'Gibbsii' which has the largest berries of any tree in the garden, but to be seen for only a few days as they are most attractive to blackbirds; there is also a profusion of shrubs including several moyesii type roses. The open area (35) we now approach is where the large beech trees were removed in 1977. It is all, of course, newly planted, with mainly ericacious and coniferous plants. At the crossing there is a good view of the ruins with the Lion Summerhouse and the house in the background. Between the *C. lawsoniana* 'Kilmacurragh' to the right of the obelisk and the Norway maple *Acer platanoides* 'Schwedleri' behind the wall is another variety of *Sequoia sempervirens* called 'Adpressa' which is now assuming a tree-like shape. On the right of the path between you and the bay laurel, *Laurus nobilis,* the Laurel of the ancients, is *Camellia x williamsii* 'J. C. Williams' which is doing well completely exposed following the removal of the beeches. Now turn left, then right into the ruin, and note on the left the flat-topped Lawson's cypress 'Tabuliformis'. We hope to keep an interesting collection of small plants in the ruin (36). Beyond the ruin there are many plants including several varieties of ivy. Ahead is the Lion Summerhouse (37) converted from the old lavatory in December 1978. Round about it we hope to grow sun-loving plants such as cistus, escallonia, hebe, halimium, etc, bearing in mind the greedy lime roots. The path on the right before you come to the summer-house used to be under heavy shade from the beeches, and the hedges of *Mahonia aquifolium* were planted in the hope that they would thrive under the poor conditions; they are layers or seedlings from plants in the garden. On the right was a large deep hollow which we had dug to make the heather hill and subsequently filled in with weeds and soil. There are some interesting rhododendrons, pieris, *Enkianthus campanulatus* 'Alba', *Berberis linearifolia,* and a hybrid of it, and many herbaceous plants including *Euphorbia griffithii* 'Fireglow', *E. sikkimensis, E. polychroma,* lilies, hemerocallis and irises, and a young *Magnolia sieboldii* 'Charles Coates'.

Back to the Doulton urn (8) we this time turn sharp left towards the summer-house (1) through what we call the old wood. This has always been a difficult site because of lime roots, couch and honey fungus. As it is a mass of snowdrops, crocuses, daffodils and bluebells it has been very difficult to find the right time to get rid of the couch without destroying many of the bulbs. On the right past the snake bark maple is *Hamamelis mollis* 'Brevipetala', then further in *Koelreuteria paniculata* and still further back the charming *Camellia* 'Cornish Snow'. The young magnolia with the large leaves is *M. officinalis biloba* and in front of it near the path *M. wilsonii*. The fastigiate oak next to it

172   *Cistus cyprius* in the ruin with the dwarf
Viburnum opulus 'Nanum' in front

has had toadstools of the honey fungus growing on it, but seems healthy enough. At the end of the path the tree with the copper bark is *Prunus maackii*. On the way into the splendid yew (38) note the round leaved rhododendron *R. orbiculare* on the right. When we came in 1957 we were not aware of this yew as it was surrounded by large twiggy sweet chestnuts which we removed after a few years. To the right of the yew is the interesting winter-flowering shrub *Stachyurus praecox* which flowers in late winter or early spring. On the other side of the yew is the small *Rhododendron* 'Yellow Hammer'. Now we are back in the front garden (39) by the fine *Chamaecyparis lawsoniana* 'Lutea' planted in 1959. It was planted in the middle of the lawn and we have gradually extended the beds all round it. The *Magnolia liliiflora* 'Nigra' was brought from our London garden in 1957 and we have several layers from it. This part is predominantly heathers and small conifers; started in 1970 it is chronologically our fifth 'heather garden'. The first was made in 1958 near the square (30), the next in front of the tree heaths we saw from the tower, in 1963, also in 1963 the heather hill which is now the ruin, then the sweep (32) in 1967, this one in 1970, and lastly in the beech area in 1978.

Between the magnolia and the steps note the pink foliage of the *C. v.* 'Mrs Pat', the spreading *Daboecia cantabrica* 'Praegerae' with large pink flowers, the clump of *E. cinerea* 'C. D. Eason', and the grey leaved *C. v* 'Silver Queen'. Standing by the sundial looking to the Doulton urn note the 'avenue' of small conifers with low heathers in between. There is good autumn colour from the group of Japanese maples *Acer ginnala, Acer palmatum* and the azaleas to the left of the large yew.

Walking up towards the twisted willow and stopping half way (40), the trees in the border on the right starting from the bottom are *Ptelea trifoliata* 'Aurea', *Magnolia stellata,* a *Picea omorika* (the Pagoda tree) and behind it *Cupressus macrocarpa* 'Goldcrest' (1971), *Cornus nuttallii, Magnolia x soulangiana* 'Rustica Rubra' (could be 'Lennei'), and *Ptelea trifoliata* 'Aurea'. There are in front many herbaceous and bulbous plants including *Hosta* 'Thomas Hogg', *Liatris* 'Kobold', pink bergamot (monarda) *Lilium tigrinium, L. pardalinum* and the biennial caper spurge (*Euphorbia lathyrus*).

And so back to the summer-house after a tour of most of the garden during which I have mentioned just about 300 different trees and shrubs. In February 1980 my wife and I went round and counted about 1,150 different trees and shrubs in 240 genera, including 200 heathers but not including named and unnamed azaleas and hybrid tea roses. This seems quite a lot but not so many when you think of Hillier's *Manual* which has over 8,000 in 638 genera. We will never begin to compete with that and fortunately it is quite unnecessary in a private garden. Some figures extracted from *The Garden* of March 1980 may also be of interest. Of about a quarter of a million higher plant species in the whole world there are about 11,500 found in Europe and less than 2,000 in Britain. There are also cultivated in Britain in addition over 8,000 species from all over the temperate world plus over 20,000 cultivars. We will go on planting, particularly small trees and shrubs. Of herbaceous and bulbous plants we have several hundred and there are many more in nurseries, large and small, if one takes the trouble to look for them.

Above: *Phlomis russelliana* with one of our most
ubiquitous and favourite shrubs, *Rosa rubrifolia*

Below: *Astrantia major* 'Rubra' in front of the dwarf
Lawson's cypress 'Pygmaea Argentea' in the ruin

Above: *Camellia* 'Cornish snow'

Below: Azaleas and *Rhodododendron* 'Helen Schiffner'
near the tea terrace

Appendix I

SIR JOHN HOWELL'S WILL

In the name of God Amen: I Sir John Howell of Wrotham in the County of Kent Knight on the eleventh day of June in the seventeenth year of the reign of our Soveraign Lord Charles by the grace of God King of England Scotland France and Ireland defender of the faith Anno Dom 1641: being aged sickly in body and of sound and perfect memory do make and ordain this my last will and testament in manner and form following first I bequeath my soul into the hands of God my only Saviour Jesus Christ who gave it hoping and believing the free pardon of all my sins and remission of the punishment due for the same through his precious death and blud sheding And my body I commend to the earth from whence it was taken; item I give unto the poor the sum of fifty pounds of and good and lawfull mony of England viz forty pounds to the poor of the parish of Wrotham, whereof I will and apoynt twenty pounds to be disbursed at the discretion of my executrix hereafter named upon the day of my buriall to such persons as my said executrix shall consider to have most need, and the other twenty pounds to be divided in like manor on that day twelve month, the other ten pounds I will to be distributed to the poor of other parishes as shall report to the church at the day of my buriall. Item I do give unto my brother Sir John Clarke Knight, to my Neice Cisely Dame Swann the daughter of the said Sir John Clarke Knight, to my nephew Richard Leah Esqr to my Brother and sister Doc: Cheeke and his wife, to my sister Dorothy Clarke, to my Brother Thomas Brodnax Esqr, and Mrs Jane Brodnax his wife and to every of them one ring of gold at the value of forty shillings. And I do entreat them in love to accept these small tokens of my best affection and to wear them for my sake. Item I do give unto my nephew John Luck the son of my sister Ann the sum of an hundred pounds of lawfull English mony to be paid unto him the said John Luck within one year after my decease provided always and my meaning is that if the said John Luck shall refuse to seal and deliver a general release to mine executrix at the time of the above appointed payment of the said hundred pounds whereby he the said John Luck shall wholly exclude himself his heirs and assignees from interrupting by any claim or sute of law that course which I have settled in every part of my estate, then only the sum of five pounds shall be paid unto the said John Luck and no more. Item I give unto every one of the other children of my said sister Ann and to every of the children of my sister Constance the sum of five pounds apiece of good and lawfull mony of England so many as shall be living at the time of my death to be payd within one year after the time of my decease; Item I give unto Mr. Charles Hutchinson now vicar of Wrotham aforesaid, to Mr. John Grime now parson of Ightham, Mr. Richard Bowles now minister of the Parish of Shipbourne, to my cousin Mr. Francis Cornwell late vicar of Horton Kirby all within the aforesaid county of Kent the sum of five pounds apiece to be paid to every of them within the space of three months after my decease. Item I give and bequeath unto Elizabeth Howell als Luck the daughter of my nephew Edward Howell als Luck the sum of five hundred pounds of lawful English money to be

Red bergamot with the grass *Stipa gigantea* behind, and *Liatris* 'Kobold' just coming into bloom, in front

paid unto her by my said executrix her executors or administrators when she shall accomplish the age of one and twenty years if she shall then be married and if she shall not be married at the said age then my meaning is that the said five hundred pounds shall be paid unto her by my said executrix her executors or administrators within seven months after the day of her marriage. Item I give unto the three children of my nephew Mr. Edward Howell als Luck viz. Mary Edward and Charles the sums of five pounds apiece of good and lawfull mony of England within the space of three months after my decease provided always that if any of my legataries within named shall sue molest or trubble with any suites in law mine executrix hereafter to be named about the probate or execution of this my last will and testament excepting the lawful recoveries of such legacies as are therein expressed then all such legacies as are severally bequeathed shall be utterly void and of none effect and every such person unduly so vexing and molesting to have twelve pence only and no more. Item I give unto every one of my household servants that shall have served me the space of one whole year before the day of my decease to every one of them twenty shillings for every several year that they shall have served me at the time of my death (that is to say) severally so many pounds as they shall severally have served me years whether they shall have served me more than a year or less than a year according to the portion of the time to be paid to them within one whole year after my decease. Item I give to my loving wife Dame Sarah Howell the sum of an hundred pounds a year for the increase of her joynture. I give unto my nephew Mr. Edward Howell als Luck the sum of one hundred pounds a year for the education of the children which he had by his former wife my neice Mrs. Frances Paris to be had and recovered out of all my lands or leases whatsoever. Item I give and bequeath unto my said wife Dame Sarah Howell all my goods debts chattels and moveables whatsoever excepting my plate and household stuff which I will unto her during the time she remains my widow promising that she will carefully preserve it and leave it to my nephew John Howell als Luck the sonne of my nephew Edward Howell als Luck and also excepting my leases which I give unto my said wife until she shall have raised such sum or sums as she shall stand charged withall either of debts legacies or funeral charges out of my said goods debts leases or other movables. After I will those my said leases to my nephew John Luck his heirs administrators and assignes which said Dame Sarah my wife I make and ordain sole executor of this my last will and testament And this is the last will and testament of me the said Sir John Howell Knight concerning the deposition of all my lands and tenements as well freehold and copy the day and year above written: I give all my lands and tenements in Kent and in Sussex as well freehold as copy to my nephew John Howell als Luck the son of my nephew Edward Howell als Luck and to the heirs male of his body lawfully begotten and in default of such issue to his brother Robert Howell als Luck and the heirs male of his body lawfully begotten and for default of such issue to his brother William Howell als Luck and the heirs male of his body lawfully begotten and in default of such issue to his brother Richard Howell als Luck. Provided always that if it should so fall out that my said wife Dame Sarah Howell should be with child at the time of my death and have a sonne I bequeath all my lands and leases unto my sonne, but if it happened that she should have a daughter then I will and bequeath her the sum of two thousand pounds of lawfull mony of England to be payd unto her out of the aforesaid lands and leases, and to be equally raised out of the valuation of the said lands and leases at the time of her marriage or when she shall obtain the full age of one and twenty years, and my lands and leases to go as formerly bequeathed. And this I declare to be the last will and testament of me the said Sir John Howell Knight and I do hereby renounce all other wills formerly made and declared. In witness whereof I have set my hand and seal given the day and year above written: sealed published and declared in these two sheets of paper to be the last will and testament of me the above said Sir John Howell Knight and hereby all former wills and testaments by me made and declared utterly renounced and revoked.   John Howell.

In the presence of us whose names are hereunder written
John Grime   John Whitehouse   Robert Woodden

Whereas I have by my last will and testament above written bequeathed to my nephew Mr. Edward Howell als Lucke the sum of one hundred pounds per annum of good and lawfull mony of England to be payd out of all my lands and tenements towards the education and provision of those children which he had as above specified had by his first wife my neice Mrs. Frances Paris I do further declare that my will and testament is that he shall enjoy the said hundred pounds per annum during the term of his natural life to be payd him at two equall payments (viz) fifty pounds every half year (viz) at the two usual feasts of St. Michael the Archangell and fifty pounds at ye feast of the Annunciation of the blessed Virgin to begin at the feast next following after my decease And if it should happen that the said Edward Howell als Lucke should depart this world before the death of my wife then my will is that my nephew John Howell als Lucke the elder sonne of my said nephew Edward Howell als Lucke aforesaid shall have and enjoy the said hundred pounds a yeare towards his own maintenance and other brothers and sisters during the naturall life of my said wife Dame Sarah in manor and form as above said to be leased out of all my lands tenements and leases whatsoever by any legal course In witness whereof I have set my hand and seal   John Howell

Sealed and delivered in the presence of us   John Grimes
          John Whitehouse   Robert Woodden

Proved at London the fourth day of September 1641

Appendix II

Some of the books and articles consulted

H. F. Abell	Kent in the Civil War.
W. J. Bean	Trees and Shrubs Hardy in the British Isles.
J. Brown	Modern Strathaven with Peeps at its Past.
P. Cane	The Creative Art of Garden Design.
J. M. Cowan	George Forrest Journeys and Plant Introductions.
E. H. M. and P. A. Cox	Modern Rhododendrons.
W. F. Downie	A History of Strathaven and Avondale.
Sir John Dunlop	The Pleasant Town of Sevenoaks.
C. Eley	Twentieth Century Gardening.
H. N. Ellacombe	In a Gloucestershire Garden.
A. M. Everett	The Community of Kent in the Great Rebellion 1641/60
C. H. Fielding	Memories of Malling and its Valleys.
R. Gorer	Living Tradition in the Garden.
M. Hadfield	Gardening in Britain.
E. Hasted	History of the County of Kent.
M. Hawarth-Booth	Effective Flowering Shrubs.
Hillier and Sons	Hillier's Manual of Trees and Shrubs.
P. Hunt	The Shell Gardens Book.
A. J. Huxley and A. G. Healey	*The Garden*, October 1974.
W. Ingwersen	Ingwersen's Manual of Alpine Plants.
G. Jekyll	Wood and Garden.
G. Jekyll	Colour Schemes for the Flower Garden.
G. Jekyll	Home and Garden.
A. T. Johnson	A Woodland Garden.
C. Lloyd	The Well-Tempered Garden.
D. McClintock	A Guide to the Naming of Plants.
J. Newman	West Kent and The Weald.
C. E. Lucas Phillips	*Journal of the R.H.S.*, October 1970.
Platt Society	Platt and its Heritage.
W. Robinson	The English Flower Garden.
A. Scott-James	Sissinghurst. The Making of a Garden.
R. Sudell	Practical Gardening and Food Production.
G. S. Thomas	The Modern Florilegium.
G. S. Thomas	Perennial Garden Plants.
G. S. Thomas	Plants for Ground Cover.
G. S. Thomas	The Gardens of the National Trust.
G. Ward	Sevenoaks Essays.
R. M. Warnicke	William Lambarde.
Women's Institute	*Home and Country,* May 1965.
Women's Institute	*West Kent News*, August 1955.
T. Wright	The Gardens of Britain, Kent, East and West Sussex and Surrey.
G. Yates	A Pocket Guide to Heather Gardening.

The Concise Oxford Dictionary of Quotations.

Index

Illustrations are indicated by the page number appearing in italic type

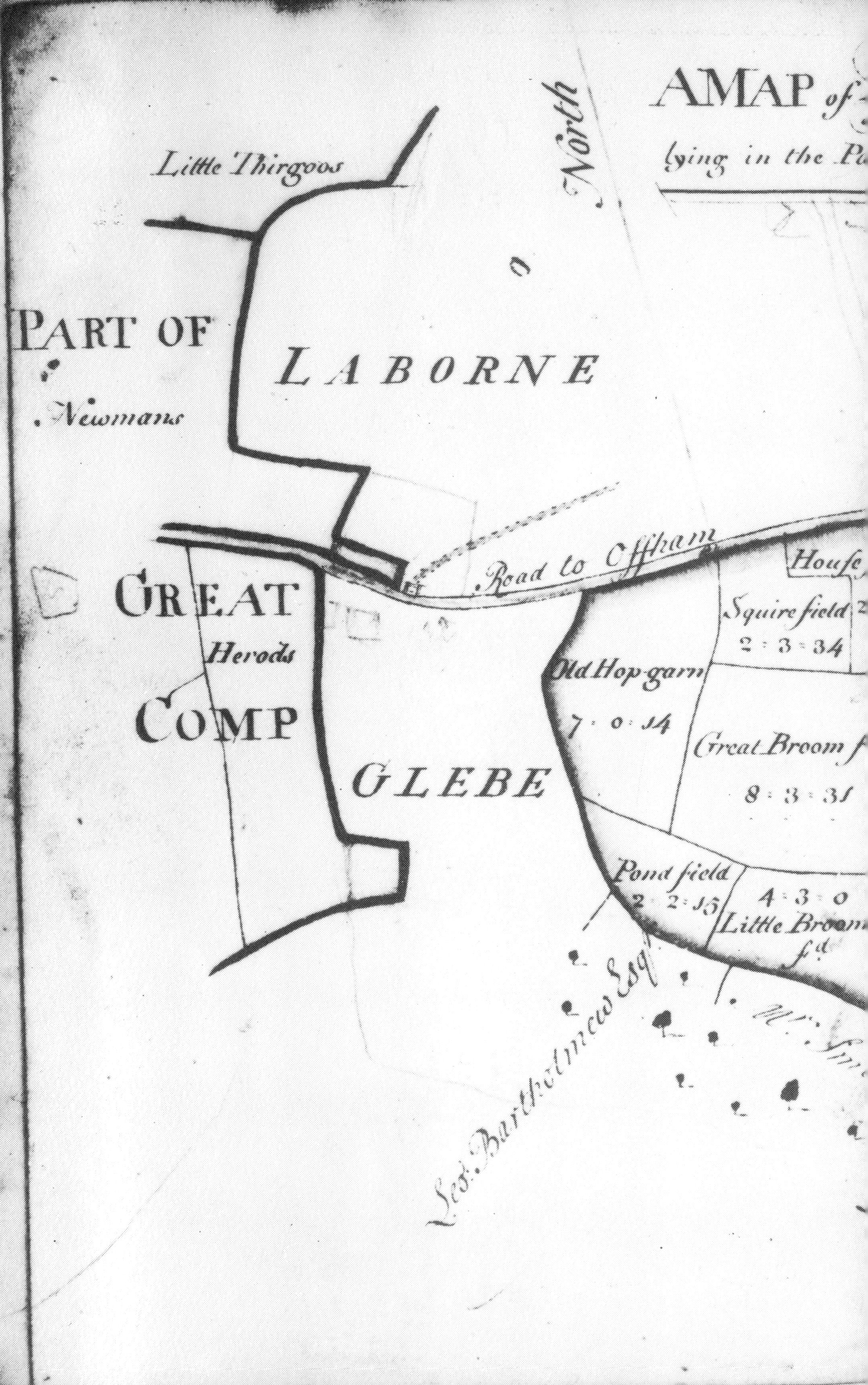

A MAP of
lying in the Pa

Little Thirgoos

North

PART OF

LABORNE

. *Newmans*

Road to Offham

House

GREAT

Squire field
2 . 3 . 34

Herods

Old Hop garn
7 . 0 . 14

COMP

Great Broom f
8 . 3 . 31

GLEBE

Pond field
2 . 2 . 15

4 . 3 . 0
Little Broom
f.d

Jes. Bartholomew Esq.